THE GREAT BRITISH
BAKE OFF ®
─ BAKE IT BETTER ─

SWEET BREAD
& BUNS

Linda Collister

HODDER &
STOUGHTON

Contents

BAKE IT BETTER
Baker's Guide

BAKE IT BETTER
Recipes

Easy does it   34

Needs a little skill 106

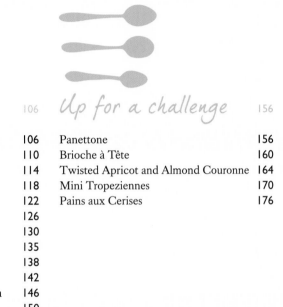

Up for a challenge 156

Welcome bakers!

This book gives you 40 great recipes for sweet bread and buns, which explain and show all the techniques you need to become a better baker. Starting with the key skills of mixing, kneading, proving, shaping and baking, recipes move you gently on to enriching with butter, incorporating fruit or nuts, and more complex shaping and finishing techniques.

Start with the 'Easy does it' section, then, as you become more confident you'll be ready to move on to the 'Needs a little skill' section. The 'Up for a challenge' recipes are the real showstoppers, perfect for weekend baking projects or to show off your bread-making skills: try the Twisted Apricot and Almond Couronne, for example, or the complex Pains aux Cerises.

The colour strip on the right-hand side of the page is your guide to the level of difficulty of the recipe: one spoon for the easiest, up to three for the more complex and challenging. It also lists any special equipment needed, as well as giving an indication of the hands-on and baking times you will need to allow (plus resting and rising times). But before you start to bake, take a look at the Baker's Guide at the beginning of the book as this will give you a head start. It explains in more detail the terms and techniques used in the recipes, as well as the most important ingredients and essential equipment you'll need.

Bread can be simple – a warm scone topped with jam and cream; a slice of toast – or it can be the centrepiece of special meal, but every loaf can taste and look impressive. With *Bake It Better: Sweet Bread & Buns* you can learn to bake like a pro, so now's the time to get out the flour, start baking and show off those skills!

HOW TO USE THIS BOOK

SECTION 1: BAKER'S GUIDE
Read this section before you start baking. The Baker's Guide contains key information on ingredients (pages 10–15), equipment (pages 16–19) and skills (pages 20–29) relevant to the recipes in the book.

Refer back to the Baker's Guide when you're baking if you want a refresher on a particular skill. In the recipes the first mention of each skill is highlighted in bold.

SECTION 2: THE RECIPES
Colour strips on the right-hand side and 1, 2 or 3 spoons show the level of difficulty of the recipe. Within the colour strips you'll find helpful information to help you decide what to bake: Hands-on time; Hands-off time; Baking time; Makes/Serves; Special equipment and Storage.

Refresh your knowledge of any essential skills by referring to the Baker's Guide before you get started.

Refer back to the Baker's Guide when a skill is highlighted in bold in the recipe if you need a reminder.

Try Something Different options are given where the recipe lends itself to experimenting with ingredients or decorations.

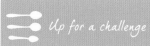

BAKE IT BETTER

Baker's Guide

Ingredients

All you really need for most of the recipes in this book are flour, yeast, salt, water and something to sweeten the dough – maybe some sugar, honey or maple syrup. Add in a few extras – nuts, dried fruit or chocolate – and you can completely change your bread very easily. Here are a few guidelines to keep in mind when buying, storing and using your ingredients.

BAKING POWDER, BICARBONATE OF SODA AND CREAM OF TARTAR

Some sweet breads need the help of a chemical raising agent to increase their lightness. The two most common are **bicarbonate of soda** (an alkali) and **cream of tartar** (an acid). **Baking powder** is a mixture of both. Raising agents work by reacting together with moisture and heat to release small bubbles of carbon dioxide, which lighten the crumb of your bake. Some recipes, such as the Soda Bread on page 38, use a slightly acidic ingredient, such as buttermilk or yoghurt, in combination with bicarbonate of soda to produce the bubbles of gas (see page 13 for more information on buttermilk). Make sure you use the exact amount stated, and discard out-of-date or damp raising agents as they won't give you the best bake. To check if baking powder is still active mix a teaspoonful into a glass of warm water – if it bubbles up nicely it's fine to use, otherwise, throw it out.

BUTTER

Most bakers use **unsalted butter**, which has a lovely rich flavour and gives a more evenly coloured bake because it contains less whey than salted butters. Some **salted butters** also have a strong taste that can be overpowering in a sweet bake. Wrap butter well and store it in the fridge away from strong flavours, or freeze for up to a month.

Instructions are given in each recipe for whether your butter should be used at room temperature, softened or chilled. In particular, doughs that are **enriched** with butter, such as the Brioche à Tête on page 160, require the butter to be squeezed into the dough with your hands, whereas laminated doughs are made by enclosing a square of chilled butter in the dough, so it is essential to have the butter at the right temperature. Remove from the fridge in plenty of time, if necessary, so that it's the right consistency for your recipe.

CHOCOLATE

Good-quality chocolate is widely available in supermarkets and you can get chips in larger bags from online suppliers, but you can also use bars chopped into pieces.

Store bars of chocolate well wrapped in a cool, dry, dark cupboard, and away from strong-flavoured ingredients. **Dark chocolate** is most widely used in this book. One with around 70 per cent cocoa solids will give the best flavour. Anything over 75 per cent can be too dry and bitter for general baking. **Cocoa nibs** are small shards of shelled, roasted cocoa beans. They are unsweetened, and at 100 per cent cocoa, have a very intense flavour. They are an excellent way to bring flavour and a slight crunchy texture to breads, such as the Baked Mocha Doughnuts on page 92. **Cocoa powder** is a dark, unsweetened powder made from pure cocoa with nearly all the cocoa butter removed – it is very bitter and powerfully flavoured, and adds an excellent chocolate taste. Don't use drinking chocolate, which has had sugar and dried milk powder added to it, as a substitute.

DRIED FRUIT

Vine fruits, such as raisins, sultanas and currants are preserved but still soft. They add sweetness and moisture, as well as a fruity flavour. Soft-dried apricots, dates, prunes, figs, cranberries, blueberries and sour cherries can replace vine fruits in many recipes. **Candied peel** is widely available ready chopped, but can also be found as whole pieces of orange, lemon or citrus peel, allowing you to cut the pieces into a size and mix that you prefer. Store opened packets in a screw-topped jar.

EXTRACTS AND FLAVOURINGS

Avoid synthetic flavourings as they can give your bake a rather unpleasant 'fake' taste.

Vanilla extract and **almond extract** are concentrated liquids, so use them in tiny quantities. Whole **vanilla pods** are a good addition to your store cupboard, and once used you can dry them off and pop them into a jar of caster sugar. They will lightly infuse the sugar with their flavour.

Ground spices are used in many sweet bakes; cinnamon is a particular favourite and crops up in lots of recipes in this book. Mixed spice is a traditional flavouring for Hot Cross Buns (see page 60), while saffron adds a rich flavour and glorious golden colour to Cornish Saffron Buns and Swedish Lussekatts (see pages 84 and 98). Spices should be measured carefully and kept in screw-topped jars rather than open packs. It's best to buy them in small quantities so you can use them while they are still fresh.

Oranges and lemons can be zested to provide quick flavour; make sure to use unwaxed fruit.

FLOUR

Flour is probably the most important ingredient in baking, but especially so in bread-making. Poor-quality or past-its-best flour can really affect the final taste and texture of your loaf. As with all ingredients, flour should be used when fresh, so store it correctly: to stop it getting damp, keep opened packs in storage jars, plastic food boxes or plastic food bags. Don't add new flour to old and use it within a month of opening, or by its best-before date. Keep an eye on wholemeal flours and flours with added grains as they spoil quicker than refined flours, and don't use flour that smells slightly rancid or contains weevils or mites.

Wheat flours, like all flours, are defined by their rate of extraction – how much of the entire wheat grain or kernel is used in the flour. **White flour** usually contains about 75 per cent of the kernel and has most of the bran and wheatgerm removed. **Wholemeal** or **wholegrain flour** has 100 per cent extraction, which means the complete kernel is ground. The high proportion of bran in wholegrain flours – those coarse golden specks – means your loaf won't rise as well as one made with all-white flour, as the bran hinders gluten development, but the flavour and health benefits will be greater. Some wheat flours have malted wheat grains added to give a sweeter taste and slightly crunchy texture.

Wheat flour for bread-making is labelled as 'bread flour' or 'strong flour', as it contains flour milled from wheat with a higher proportion of protein to starch than that used for pastry and cakes. It is the protein content that's key to yeasted bread-making: as the dough is kneaded, the protein develops into strands of gluten, which help the dough to rise by expanding around the gases produced by the yeast. **Plain** and **self-raising flours** have 8–10 per cent protein (ideal for non-yeast breads, as well as cakes and pastries); **strong bread flour** has 12–16 per cent protein (ideal for most breads); and **extra-strong** or **extra-strong Canadian flour** has 15–17 per cent protein (ideal for bagels or larger loaves).

Rye flour was once a staple in places where the soil was too poor, or too cold, for wheat, but is now popular for its deep flavour and dark, chewy crumb. Rye flour has a low gluten content, which makes it harder to work than wheat flours, but some find it easier to digest.

Spelt flour has been grown throughout Europe for centuries. It comes from the same family as common wheat, but is more nutritious and higher in protein. Spelt flour is available as both wholegrain and 'white'.

Stoneground flour is produced when cereal grains (wheat, rye, oats, etc.) are milled between two large stones, instead of the steel rollers used for mass-produced flours. It has a different texture and fuller flavour.

Gluten-free flours are blends of wheat-free flours, usually rice, potato, chickpea, tapioca, sorghum, broad bean, maize or buckwheat, depending on the brand. (Try different brands, as they vary in flavour.) Some mixes also contain xanthan gum, which replaces gluten in giving structure to the dough. Check the label; if your mix doesn't include it, add 1 teaspoon xanthan gum per 150g flour. Gluten-free flours often need more liquid, so you can't interchange them exactly with wheat flour.

HONEY

Honey can be used as an alternative to sugar when sweetening dough, as in the Milk and Honey Loaf (see page 46). Look for honey from a single variety of flower or plant (such as orange blossom), as the flavour is often more distinct, but be careful that it doesn't overpower the flavours in your bake. As a general rule, the paler the honey, the milder the flavour. Soft-set honey (but not honeycomb) is easiest to blend in, but solid honey can be used if it is softened first (gently warm it in a microwave or in a small dish set in a bowl of hot water). Honey also adds moisture, but too much can make the mixture dense, so follow the recipe carefully.

LIQUIDS

There's no need to use bottled or spring water: tap is fine. Some bakers prefer to use filtered water that's been boiled, and cooled, to remove any chlorine – this is most relevant for sourdoughs because chlorine can hinder growth of the cultures. Many recipes replace some, or all, of the water with other ingredients, such as the Muesli Round on page 64, where the liquid element is provided by soaking oats in apple juice. Make sure you add liquids at the temperature stated in the recipe; if they are too warm they will kill the yeast.

Milk gives the bread a finer, softer crumb. **Cream** or **Jersey high-fat milk** is used where a rich, heavy dough is required, as in the Swedish Lussekatts on page 98. It is also used to make crème pâtissière (see Pains aux Cerises, page 177).

Yoghurt is often added to breads as it helps fermentation and flavour. **Buttermilk** is fermented a bit like yoghurt. It is used to raise non-yeast doughs, such as the Sweet Soda Bread (see page 38). Both are slightly acidic, which helps lighten the dough when combined with an alkali ingredient.

Eggs add flavour and enrich dough, but make it slightly heavier, too. They also add colour, like the golden shade of brioche. The recipes in this book use medium-sized eggs (62–65g each). Their size is important as they work in ratio with the other ingredients. Using a different-sized egg may affect results – you may need more liquid, or the dough may not bind together well, rise properly or cook all the way through.

Store eggs in the fridge, pointed-side down, to protect the yolk from drying out and spoiling. Keep them in the box they came in and in the cooler body of the fridge, not the door, and use by the best before date. Spare egg whites freeze well for up to a month – mark the quantity and date on the container and defrost thoroughly before use.

MARGARINE AND SPREADS
Margarines are based on vegetable oils, with added salt and flavourings. Some are made specifically for baking and can be used straight from the fridge. They give good results but won't taste the same as bakes made with butter. Spreads designed for use on breads and crackers are not meant for baking and won't give a good bake as they contain too much water and not enough fat.

NUTS
All sorts of nuts, such as **walnuts, pecans, hazelnuts, almonds, pistachios** and **macadamia nuts**, can be added to your dough with the flour, or kneaded in towards the end. Lightly toasting them first in a dry frying pan will increase their flavour.

Nuts are not usually added as a topping as they burn too easily to cope with the high oven temperatures. Because of their high oil content, check nuts taste fresh before using.

OILS
Some recipes use **light olive, sunflower** or **rapeseed oil**, all of which have a mild, neutral flavour and should not be confused with **vegetable oil**, a frying oil which will give a distinctive, unpleasant 'savoury' flavour to your baking. Oil is used in traditional dairy-free breads, such as the Poppy Seed Challah on page 114. Oil makes the dough moist and soft so it keeps for longer, but too much will make the dough very heavy and greasy.

SALT
The recipes in this book use fine sea salt; if you have the coarser, flaked sort, crush it first so that it combines easily with the flour. Salt is added to bread not only for flavour, but also for its role in the development of the dough structure. Most recipes use 1–2g salt per 100g flour. When adding salt, keep it out of contact with the yeast for as long as possible as salt slows down yeast growth.

SUGAR
It's important to use the type of sugar specified in the recipe as they all behave in slightly different ways. Store in airtight jars or bags to stop them from drying out.

Caster sugar is refined white sugar with a fine texture, making it ideal for most general baking, as it incorporates easily into your mixtures and combines well with butter. **Golden caster sugar** is less refined than caster sugar, giving it a pale golden colour and a slightly richer flavour. **Granulated**

sugar takes longer to dissolve and can leave a speckled appearance on top of your bakes.

Demerara sugar is often sprinkled on top of sweet buns to create a crisp, sweet crust (see Cornish Saffron Buns, page 84).

Soft light brown sugar or **light and dark muscovado sugar** add a stronger caramel taste, and are used when a warmer butterscotch or caramel taste is wanted. They can form into lumps during storage, so sift or press the lumps out before using.

White icing sugar is used after baking to dust sweet loaves like Stollen and Kugelhopf (see pages 130 and 142); **golden unrefined icing sugar** won't give the same dramatic snowy contrast to the golden brown crust. **Fondant icing sugar** is a ready-prepared mix of icing sugar and powdered glucose syrup that can be mixed with water or fruit juice to make an icing that sets firm.

Pearl sugar is fine nibs of sugar used to decorate the tops of small buns and loaves, rather than added to a dough.

SYRUPS AND OTHER SWEETENERS

Golden syrup is a sticky, pale gold syrup made from sugar cane sap. It's sweeter than sugar and helps keep breads moist and easier to slice. **Maple syrup** is the boiled-down sap of sugar maple trees and has a wonderful red-gold colour and unsurpassed flavour. It is expensive, and beware cheaper 'maple-flavour' syrups that won't produce the same results. **Malt extract** is a delicious by-product of the brewing industry, made from malted barley grains mixed with water. It gives a wonderful, sweet flavour to Sticky Malted Loaf (see page 78). Syrups can be messy to measure, so sit the whole tin in a bowl of just-boiled water, or warm the measuring spoon in a mug of boiled water.

YEAST

Yeast is the living organism that makes bread rise. It needs moisture, gentle warmth and flour (or sugar) to stimulate growth and the production of carbon dioxide, which expands the dough. These recipes use dried powdered yeast, sold in 7g sachets as fast-action, easy-blend or instant dried yeast. They must be kept in a cupboard. The powder must be added to the flour and dry ingredients (never to liquid). Hot water kills yeast, while salt slows its growth.

Fresh yeast is greyish-brown, with a distinct aroma, and feels like clay. It can be stored, tightly wrapped, in a sealed plastic box in the fridge for a week, but should be used before it turns dark brown or powdery grey. Use 15g fresh yeast instead of a 7g sachet fast-action dried yeast; crumble it into a bowl and cream it to a smooth liquid with about 7 tablespoons of your measured liquid, then work in a little of the measured flour and leave for about 15 minutes. When it froths and bubbles it is ready to use – add to the flour and dry ingredients with the rest of the liquid. If your mixture isn't frothy, it's not working. Some dried yeast, sold as 'regular dried yeast', needs to be mixed with a little measured lukewarm liquid and sugar, and left for 15 minutes to 'froth up' before adding to the flour with the remaining liquid – check the pack for instructions.

Use the quantity of yeast specified in the recipe; use more and the dough will be lively but the loaf may have a strong aftertaste and keep less well; use less and the dough will take longer to rise and prove, but have a deeper flavour.

Equipment

You don't need lots of fancy equipment for bread-making, but good-quality essentials will make your life easier and give you more consistent results. Here is our list of the basics, plus a few extra bits of kit you might find useful.

BAKING PAPER
Non-stick baking paper and **parchment paper** are best for lining baking sheets and trays. **Greaseproof paper** has a waxy coating that doesn't stand up so well to the heat of the oven.

BAKING SHEETS AND TRAYS
Baking sheets have only one raised edge for gripping, which means you'll be able to slide your bread on and off it easily. Baking trays have sides all the way round. Buy at least one very heavy-duty sheet that won't buckle or warp in a really hot oven.

BISCUIT CUTTERS
A nest of cutters in various sizes is ideal for cutting out individual bakes like scones and doughnuts (see pages 34 and 92). Metal cutters will give you the cleanest edge.

BOWLS
If you're buying new, a nest of small, medium and large bowls is ideal. For versatility, sturdiness (without being overly heavy) and durability, **heatproof glass** and **stainless steel** are good choices. They can be used for both cold and hot mixtures (such as when making crème pâtissière). Be aware, though, that stainless steel is not suitable for the microwave. **Plastic** bowls are cheaper and some have a built-in rubber base to help reduce wobble, although you can stabilise any bowl by placing a damp cloth underneath it. Plastic bowls are, however, quite lightweight and do feel less sturdy to work with. **Ceramic** bowls are pretty and can go in the dishwasher, but they break quite easily and can be heavy. **Anodised aluminium** bowls are very durable and will last a lifetime, but they can't go in the microwave. A very large bowl with a snap-on lid is extremely useful for mixing and rising large batches of dough.

CLINGFILM OR TEA TOWELS
For covering dough and proving loaves. Use a clean, dry tea towel each time.

COOLING RACKS
A large wire cooling rack with legs is essential to let air circulate underneath cooling bread, preventing condensation and the dreaded 'soggy bottom'. You can improvise with a grill-pan rack, but the finer wires on a cooling rack are more effective.

DOUGH SCRAPER
This is one of the cheapest, but definitely most useful pieces of kit for a bread maker. It should be sturdy but flexible, so that you can scoop or scrape up doughs (and clean bowls), as well as divide them for shaping.

FREE-STANDING MIXER OR FOOD-PROCESSOR
If you do a lot of baking, a large free-standing mixer or food-processor with an attachment for making dough will save a lot of time and energy. If possible, buy an extra bowl, as it helps when batch-baking, and a snap-on lid is a great help for rising and/or chilling doughs.

HEAVY-DUTY OVEN GLOVES
These are vital when baking bread and must always be kept dry. Don't ever use a damp

tea towel for loading/unloading the oven, as you can burn yourself.

KNIVES

A **small, very sharp knife** is used to slash the tops of some loaves before baking, while a **large sharp knife** is vital for chopping nuts and general slicing (as is a **knife sharpener**). A **round-bladed knife** is handy for cutting up butter, and for **rubbing in**. A **long-bladed serrated bread knife** is essential for slicing baked loaves, and **kitchen scissors** are useful for snipping the tops of loaves and rolls instead of slashing. A **croissant rolling cutter** is relatively inexpensive and will make shaping croissants (see page 150) much easier.

MEASURING JUGS

Pick a heat-resistant and microwave-safe jug with both metric and imperial measures, starting from 50ml or 100ml, and going up to 2 litres. A small jug or cup that measures from 1 teaspoon (5ml) up to 4 tablespoons (60ml) is a very useful extra. And remember that you can weigh water as well as measure its volume: 1ml = 1 gram. Some bakers prefer this method as it is the most precise.

MEASURING SPOONS

A set of measuring spoons is essential for measuring small amounts of liquids and dry ingredients such as salt and spices. Day-to-day teaspoons, dessertspoons and tablespoons can vary enormously in size and will give inconsistent results. Measuring spoons range from 1/8 teaspoon to 1 1/2 tablespoons. Go for spoons with narrow ends that will fit into fiddly spice jars. Unless otherwise indicated, all spoon measures in these recipes are level – skim off any excess with a finger or the back of a knife.

OVEN THERMOMETER

Oven thermostats can be notoriously unreliable so use an oven thermometer to double-check your oven is the correct temperature and work out where the hot and cool spots are located.

PASTRY BRUSH

Pick a good-quality brush in a medium width for brushing on glazes or brushing away excess flour. Make sure it is heat resistant and dishwasher-proof.

PIPING BAGS

Disposable plastic piping bags in various sizes are available from most supermarkets and are used in this book mainly to decorate the breads, as in the Hot Cross Buns (see page 60). They are sometimes used with **piping nozzles**. Generally piping bags with non-slip exteriors are easiest to use. You can also find reusable **nylon piping bags** from specialist shops and suppliers. They are a little stronger and don't have seams for the mixtures to leak through. Most can be rinsed and then washed inside out in very hot water. Always make sure they are completely dry before putting them away.

ROLLING PIN

Choose a long, fairly heavy one about 6–7cm in diameter; ones without handles are generally easier to use. Never leave it soaking in washing-up water and don't put it in the dishwasher.

SCALES

Baking is a science, so it pays to be accurate. As you'll be dealing with some quite small quantities, **digital scales** are preferable to **spring** or **balance** scales as they are much more precise and can weigh ingredients that are as little as 1g. You can add multiple items to one bowl simply by resetting the balance to zero after adding each ingredient. Keep a spare pair of batteries handy!

SIEVE
Essential for removing lumps from sugars and other ingredients, as well as for straining soaked fruit mixtures. A stainless steel wire sieve with a large bowl is the most versatile and should last longer than plastic. A smaller tea strainer-sized sieve is also useful for dusting bakes with icing sugar.

STORAGE CONTAINERS
Most sweet breads should be eaten the day they are baked, but larger loaves should be stored in a special bread bin or cake tin, rather than a sealed plastic box, as these can encourage the bread to sweat and turn mouldy. Store well away from sources of heat (radiators/sunlight/kitchen light fittings/fridge or cooker areas) as this encourages mould to develop.

TIMER
A digital kitchen timer with seconds as well as minutes and with a loud bell, is essential. Set it for a few minutes less than the suggested time in the recipe, especially if you are unsure of your oven temperature – you can always increase the cooking time.

TINS
Always select the correct size of tin, then wash and dry it carefully before you start. A good-quality heavy-duty tin should bake without scorching or warping in the heat of the oven, stay rust-free and last a lifetime.

Loaf tins are essential for making neat, brick-shaped breads. They're available in a variety of sizes – 900g (about 26 × 12.5 × 7.5cm) is the most-used size. Silicone types won't give a good crust and can be difficult to handle when filled with heavy dough.

Deep round sandwich tins are used for softer doughs, to keep them 'confined'. A 20cm diameter tin is the most useful to start off with. A rectangular **brownie tin** will come in handy for baking pull-apart breads, such as the Chelsea Buns on page 110.

Springclip tins are deep metal tins with a spring release, a base that clamps in place when the clip is fastened, and a metal ring which lifts off when unclipped – they're mainly used for cake-making but are also useful for baking pull-apart rolls.

Specialist tins are useful for recipes such as the Baked Mocha Doughnuts on page 92, for which you'll need a **doughnut mould tray**. **Muffin tins**, usually with 12 holes, make it possible to bake individual buns. The Kugelhopf, Panettone and Brioche à Tête (see pages 142, 156 and 160) also use specialist tins. However, it is often possible to use standard tins instead (see the individual recipes for instructions on adapting regular tins). Although not technically a tin, a **non-stick crumpet ring** will help you create the perfect shape, and allows you to lift the cooked crumpet out of the pan easily (see page 44).

WOODEN SPOON
Wooden spoons are heat-resistant so are ideal for stirring mixtures over heat. It's a good idea to keep ones for baking separate from those that are used for savoury cooking, as they can absorb strong flavours.

Skills

Once your ingredients and equipment are lined up, you're ready to start baking some delicious sweet bread and buns!

The recipes in this book are designed to take you from absolute beginner to baking your own showstoppers. All the recipes tell you exactly what to do stage-by-stage, but you'll notice that some of the terms in the recipe methods are highlighted in bold. This means there's additional information about them in this section if you want to find out a bit more detail or to refresh your memory.

From mixing and kneading your dough to checking that your sweet bread and buns are properly cooked, this is the place to start, whether you're completely new to baking or want to pick up a few expert tips.

HOW TO MIX THE DOUGH

The key thing to remember when mixing dough is that you need to keep your yeast alive. Yeast (see page 15) is a simple living organism and is easily killed, by salt in particular. Weigh out your flour and put it in your mixing bowl, then mix in the salt and any sugar, spices, dried flavourings (like cocoa powder), nuts, dried fruit or raising agents as instructed in the recipe, before adding the yeast last – this is to ensure that the yeast doesn't come into direct contact with the other ingredients. Give it a stir before adding the liquids, which may include honey, eggs, oil or liquid flavourings (such as vanilla or almond extract). Many yeasted dough recipes specify lukewarm milk or water, and if they do, it's important that the liquid is not too hot or it could kill the yeast. Dip your little finger into it: it should feel just comfy. Mix it all together and **work** the liquids in with a wooden spoon, your hand – using it like a paddle – or the dough hook attachment of a large free-standing mixer on the slowest speed. Use a dough scraper to get down to the bottom of the bowl, so that your ingredients are fully mixed together (see photo, left).

You will find that many of the bakes in this book actually have fruit and nuts that are incorporated *after* the dough has been mixed and left to rise. These are usually very rich doughs that need extra time for the yeast to get going and raise the dough before the heavy ingredients are added.

Some breads, such as scones and some plainer or firmer doughs, have butter worked into the flour before the yeast and liquid is added. To do this, add the chilled and diced butter to the flour and rub it in using just the tips of your fingers, until the mixture looks like fine crumbs.

How to mix a very wet dough
Some doughs are initially made by simply combining the flour, water, salt and yeast with either a round-bladed knife or your hand to make a moist and shaggy dough – it is not kneaded or 'worked' as you don't want the gluten to be developed. This is the basis of **laminated dough** (see page 23).

HOW TO KNEAD
The process of kneading ensures the yeast is evenly distributed so that your dough rises evenly. It also develops the gluten in the flour, which means the dough will rise well. The stronger the flour (meaning the more protein it contains, see page 12) the more gluten there is, and the more your dough is able to rise. Kneading develops the gluten from a tangled mass to a network of chains that stretch around the bubbles of carbon dioxide produced by the yeast. Kneading your dough properly is vital in most bread-making, the main exception being doughs that will later be **laminated**, such as for Croissants (see page 150); these should not be kneaded as developing gluten here can produce a tough result.

It can help if you let the dough **hydrate** before you knead it; leave your dough uncovered in its bowl for about 5 minutes before you start to knead and you'll find the kneading process easier because the flour will have had time to absorb the liquid properly. This makes a particular difference with wholemeal and rye flours, which often need more liquid than white flours, and are slower to hydrate. Check the consistency of the dough after you have left it to hydrate to see whether or not it needs a little more flour or water. When kneading rye or wholemeal dough, give the dough (and yourself) a break: halfway through, cover

your dough with an upturned bowl and have a rest for 5–10 minutes, then continue. Kneading in shorter bursts helps the gluten to gradually develop and strengthen.

Very soft doughs are kneaded in the bowl by slapping them up and down until the dough is stretchy – no extra flour is used, so the dough becomes more pliable and firmer but still soft. These include the cake-like Brioche à Tête and Mini Tropeziennes (see pages 160 and 170).

How to knead by hand
1. In your bowl, bring the dough together into a ball. It should be firm enough to leave the sides of the bowl clean. If it is a bit sticky, sprinkle over a little extra flour; or add a few drops of liquid if there are dry patches. Try not to add too much of either.
2. Turn out your dough onto a very lightly floured or oiled worktop (unless otherwise stated) and set a timer – most of the doughs in this book are kneaded by hand for 10 minutes but do check the recipe.
3. Hold the end nearest down with one hand and use the other hand to pull and stretch out your dough away from you, using the heel of your hand. Gather the dough back into a ball. Give the ball a quarter turn and repeat the stretching action.
4. Repeat these movements over and over until your dough begins to change in texture and appearance to feel and look smooth, glossy and very pliable, then shape your dough into a neat ball and leave to rise, as your recipe requires.

How to knead very soft doughs
Very soft doughs kneaded on a worktop can be tricky to handle, but you don't want to add a lot of extra flour or you risk drying out the dough. A plastic dough scraper will

help you lift and move the dough around; it will also help you cope with escaping ingredients, such as fruit and nuts.

Some really soft, cake-like doughs or batters, such as for the Crumpets on page 44, are best kneaded by '**slapping**' it up and down in the bowl, using your warm hand as a paddle (*see photo, top left*). Some doughs are worked until they are so stretchy they will lift off the worktop in one piece; others just until they are very smooth and stretchy, so check the instructions.

How to knead using a free-standing mixer

This will cut down the kneading time to about 4–5 minutes. Use the dough hook attachment of the mixer and set it to the slowest possible speed and be careful not to overwork the dough in the mixer; this is a real danger when using food-processors, which is why it's actually best to avoid using them for kneading. Overworking the dough may cause you to over-extend the gluten and end up with a collapsing bread with large holes in it. While it's impossible to over-knead by hand, always take care when using a mixer. You'll also need to keep an eye out for under-kneading, which can produce a loaf that's soggy, flat or dense.

How to test if the dough has been kneaded

Often called the windowpane test, this is where you take a piece of dough, roughly the size of an egg, and stretch it between your fingers to make a thin, translucent sheet (if your dough has fruit or nuts added, you will need to choose a piece without fruit or nuts in it). If it doesn't stretch out, or it tears easily, then knead it for a little while longer (*see photo, bottom left*).

HOW TO MAKE AN ENRICHED DOUGH

There are many ways to make a dough richer: replacing some or all of the water with eggs or milk, and adding fat (usually butter, but sometimes oil or lard). Because the yeast has had to work harder to leaven the heavier-than-usual mix, greater care has to be taken. Sometimes you will see that the recipe uses a bit more yeast, and the rising and proving times increase in number and/ or length to allow for slower growth.

Butter is often added after the initial dough has been made and is the correct (often very soft and sticky) consistency. For cake-like brioche and panettone doughs the butter should be the same temperature as the dough, and roughly the same consistency so it can be easily incorporated. The best way is to use your hands; their gentle warmth works perfectly as you squeeze the butter together with the dough through your fingers (*see photo, right*). Stop when you can't see any more streaks of butter. If you prefer to use a free-standing mixer, fit the paddle attachment rather than the dough hook and use the slowest speed.

Because the dough has such a high fat content, it often needs thorough chilling so it is firm enough to shape; rising and proving is often slightly different from plain doughs so do check the recipe instructions.

Learn with: Panettone (page 156) and Mini Tropeziennes (page 170)

HOW TO MAKE A LAMINATED DOUGH

This is the trickiest of all the bread-making techniques but one you can master with practice. It is used to give croissants and other Danish pastry doughs their distinctive flakiness. Often this type of dough is also

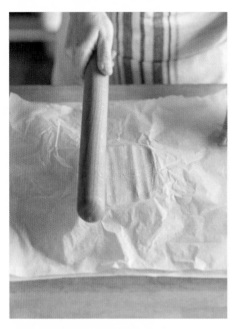

called an enriched dough, because it has a richer flavour from all the butter it uses (sometimes as much butter is used as flour, and sometimes eggs and cream are added too), but lamination actually refers to the way in which the dough is folded and layered.

What makes it so flaky rather than spongy – like a regular bread dough – is the way the butter is rolled into the dough to make hundreds of layers. The final lightness is the result of the water in the butter and the dough turning to steam in the oven and puffing up the fragile layers as it cooks.

Unlike regular yeasted doughs, it is important not to develop the gluten in the flour, as you need to avoid creating elasticity, which will prevent the layers of dough puffing up. Avoid overworking or over-stretching the dough, so it doesn't shrink rather than swell in the oven, and stick to the chilling/relaxing times given in the recipe. Don't let the butter get warm and start to ooze out of the dough, or it will be hard to handle and end up greasy and heavy. Rise and prove it in a spot that is not too warm, and in hot weather chill the dough for a little longer or use cold water to mix the dough. Keep a dry pastry brush next to the rolling pin and brush off the excess flour before folding the dough to stop the dough becoming dry and heavy.

1. **Mix** and **rise** the dough as in your recipe. Make sure it is chilled before you start the lamination process – the butter also needs to be chilled.

2. Sprinkle a little flour on the butter to be worked in, then lay it between two sheets of baking paper. Pound or beat it with a rolling pin until it is half its original thickness. Remove the baking paper, fold the butter in half, then cover with baking paper and

pound again. Keep doing this until the butter is pliable but still very cold. Beat it into square of about 10cm, or as instructed in your recipe (*see photo, page 24, top*).

3. Scoop out the chilled dough onto a floured work surface – there's no need to punch it down. With a lightly floured rolling pin, roll out in four directions to make four flaps with a thick square in the centre.

4. Put the butter, lightly dusted with flour, in the centre and fold the flaps of dough over to **enclose** it (*see photo, page 24, bottom*). Gently press the seams with the rolling pin to seal in the butter.

5. Turn the dough upside down (seams facing down) and lightly press with the rolling pin to flatten it – be careful you don't squeeze the butter out (*see photo, top right*). Wrap and chill as instructed in your recipe.

6. Gently roll out the dough to a rectangle about 54 × 18cm (or as in your recipe), then fold in three: fold the bottom third of the dough up to cover the centre third, then fold the top third down to cover the other two layers to make a neat square (*see photo, bottom right*). Lightly press the edges with the rolling pin to seal, then wrap in clingfilm and chill as instructed in your recipe before continuing. This is your first '**turn**'.

7. When the dough has chilled, lift it up and give it a quarter turn anti-clockwise so the folded, rounded, edge is by your left hand. Roll out the dough to a rectangle and fold it in three again, just as before. This is your second 'turn'. Wrap and chill the dough for an hour (or as given) then give it two more 'turns'. Wrap and chill the dough as before and continue with your recipe.

Learn with: Kouign Amann (page 138) and Croissants (page 150)

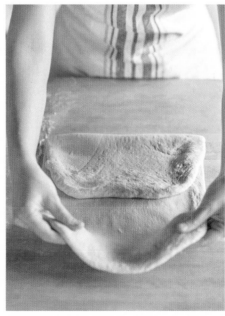

HOW TO RISE AND PROVE DOUGH

Rising is very important, as this is the time when the yeast produces the bubbles of gas that cause the dough to rise and expand. Most recipes require the dough to rise until double its original size (*see photo, left*).

Yeast likes air (which it gets from kneading), food (from the flour, sugars or other sweeteners or malt added to your dough), moisture (from the liquid in the dough, and in the atmosphere) and warmth. For the best results, bakers like to provide the dough with a moist and gently warm atmosphere so it doesn't dry out and form a skin (this will be visible in the finished loaf as a dry or tough line running through it).

A room temperature of 20–24°C (68–75°F) is ideal for rising dough. If it is left in too hot a place, the yeast will grow too rapidly and the dough can become distorted and have a slight aftertaste.

At cooler temperatures the yeast develops more slowly. Some bakers prefer slower fermentation as it results in a richer flavour and a chewy crumb, so they mix the dough with cool or chilled water and leave it to rise in a cool place, or even the fridge, overnight. With some experimentation you can also slow fermentation using less yeast.

Proving is the name given to the last rising before baking, which happens after you've shaped the dough. Some breads only have one rising/proving stage, while breads with a really fine, cake-like texture, such as the Panettone (see page 156), have multiple rises so that the gas bubbles are repeatedly broken up and become smaller and smaller.

Some of the bakes in this book don't have any rising or proving stages. These 'quick' breads rely on the chemical effects of the ingredients to produce gas bubbles to leaven the dough. Scones, baked doughnuts

and soda breads all use bicarbonate of
soda (an alkali) in combination with an
acidic ingredient, such as cream of tartar,
buttermilk or yoghurt; these instantly start
reacting to produce bubbles of gas when
combined with liquid.

**How to check if your dough is sufficiently
proved**
First look at its size. After shaping, your
dough needs to be left to prove and rise until
it has roughly doubled in size. How long
this takes will depend on the temperature of
your dough and how lively your dough is. If
it's under-proved once it goes in the oven, it
can suddenly expand in an unexpected way
and become misshapen; if over-proved, your
dough is likely to collapse in the oven as the
gluten can't cope with all the gas bubbles.
To test whether or not your dough is oven-
ready, gently prod it with your finger: if it
springs back, then it's not quite ready; if it
returns to its original shape fairly slowly, or
if there is a very slight dent (*see photo, top
right*), then it's ready. A large dent means it
is over-proved (you can sometimes save the
dough by gently kneading and reshaping,
and carefully proving again).

HOW TO KNOCK BACK AND SHAPE
Most doughs (**laminated dough** is the
exception) need to be knocked back before
shaping, and gently kneaded to redistribute
the gas bubbles. Knocking back breaks
up the large gas bubbles within the dough
so that you get smaller, finer bubbles that
will rise more evenly. Use your knuckles to
punch down your risen, puffy dough so it
collapses back to its original size (*see photo,
bottom right*); some bakers prefer to fold
the dough over on itself two or three times.
Once shaped, leave to prove before baking.

To make an oval loaf

Form the knocked back dough into an oval, then make a crease in the dough lengthways along the centre with the edge of your hand (*see photo, top left*). Roll the dough over to make a sausage (crease in the centre), then roll onto the prepared baking tray so that the seam is underneath, the top is smooth and the loaf is evenly shaped. Slash or snip the top, cover and prove before baking.

To make a tin loaf

Pat the knocked-back dough into a rectangle, with the shortest side the same length (not width) as the tin. Don't use too much flour on the work surface or you may dry out the dough and create a gap in the centre when it bakes. Brush excess flour away with a pastry brush. Roll up the dough firmly, like a Swiss roll, pinch the seam together well, then put your dough into the tin, seam-side down, usually with the ends tucked under at each end. Slash or snip the top, cover and prove before baking.

To make a round loaf

Gently knead your knocked-back dough into a ball shape. Roll the ball around under your cupped hand until it becomes smooth and neatly shaped. Set the ball on a prepared baking tray and snip or slash the top, then cover and prove before baking.

To shape small buns and breads

Small buns are shaped the same way as round loaves, by rolling a small ball of dough on the worktop under your cupped hand (*see photo, bottom left*). For doughs that are rolled out and then have shapes stamped out, such as Mini Tropeziennes (see page 170), lightly dip the cutter or sharp knife in flour before you start, and avoid dragging or stretching the dough out of shape by using short, sharp movements. For slicing up long rolls of filled dough (see Chelsea Buns, page 110), use a large and very sharp knife and a sawing motion. Clean and re-flour the knife between slices to avoid a messy result.

HOW TO TEST IF YOUR BREAD IS DONE

Carefully remove the hot bread from the oven and turn it out, upside down, into one hand (wearing heavy-duty oven gloves or using a thick, dry tea towel). Tap the underside of the loaf with your knuckles *(see photo, right)*. If the bread sounds hollow, like a drum, then the loaf is cooked through; if you just get a dull 'thud', put the bread back into the oven, directly onto the oven shelf. Bake for a few more minutes, then test again – a slightly over-baked loaf will taste far, far better than an under-baked one.

Follow the individual recipe instructions, as there are several recipes where this test does not apply – for non-yeasted breads, such as the Toasted Coconut Banana Bread (see page 40), the cocktail stick test is best: insert a cocktail stick into the middle of your bake and if it comes out clean, it is ready. Some small individual bakes like croissants and larger, sticky ones like Chelsea Buns, also have their own guide to 'doneness'.

HOW TO STORE SWEET BREAD AND BUNS

Most bakes are best eaten the same day, but some can be kept at least overnight. Wrap non-sticky cold bakes in a clean tea towel, sticky ones in baking paper, foil or clingfilm, and store in a cool spot in a bread box or cake tin. To freeze, wrap tightly in clingfilm once cold, or store in a freezer bag (or sealed plastic container) for up to 1 month.

Help!

Sometimes things go wrong in the kitchen, no matter how experienced you are, but it's not a disaster! Here are some commonly encountered bread-making problems, and our expert suggestions as to how to resolve them.

WHY DIDN'T MY DOUGH RISE?

The most obvious reason is usually to do with the yeast, so first check the expiry date on the packet – stale yeast will be ineffective. If you have used fresh yeast it may have passed its best and have died, particularly if it was left unwrapped and exposed to the air or left to dry out. See page 15 for more about fresh yeast.

If the yeast was alive and the dough still didn't rise, then the yeast must have been killed as the dough was being made. The most likely reason was exposing it to too much heat – yeast is a tiny living organism and will die at temperatures much above blood temperature, so treat it carefully and check the temperature of the water (or liquid) you are using to mix the dough: dip in your little finger, and if it feels a bit warm, replace some of the water with cold water.

When you use yeast, make sure it doesn't come into direct contact with salt or sugar as these strong, concentrated ingredients will kill it.

If you have used cold or chilled water to mix the dough, and left it to rise in a cool spot, or used less yeast than specified in the recipe, then the dough will be slower to rise (yeast thrives on gentle warmth), so be patient and move the dough to a warmer spot to encourage the yeast to grow. Remember, too, that heavy enriched doughs (those with more than usual amounts of fat, sugar and fruit) present more of a challenge for the yeast.

WHY DID MY LOAF COLLAPSE IN THE OVEN?

The usual reason is that it was left to prove (the final rising stage) for too long or in a too warm spot. If bread dough expands to more than double its original size, the gluten developed during kneading cannot expand any further to keep up with production of the bubbles of gas (from the yeast) and so eventually the structure breaks down and collapses in the heat of the oven. Always do the 'windowpane' test (see page 22) to check the dough has been sufficiently kneaded and don't rely just on the '10 minute' rule.

When you first put a loaf into a hot oven it immediately starts to rise and expand – this is the 'oven spring' caused by the gas in the dough expanding. The high heat quickly kills off the yeast and starts to set the dough, but if the oven is too cool, the yeast keeps on producing bubbles of gas and the dough keeps on expanding until the gluten can't contain it and the dough collapses.

There's not much you can do if this has happened: the loaf will taste fine but will be a bit dense and heavy, so use it toasted.

WHY IS THE DRIED FRUIT JUST AT ONE EDGE OF THE LOAF?

Adding fruit and/or nuts to a dough changes its structure – and if you add too many extra ingredients the dough will collapse under the weight of it all, so follow the recipe carefully. Make sure the fruit is evenly distributed throughout the dough by careful, thorough kneading, and it's a good idea to check the fruit mix first to break up any clumps that may have formed in the pack.

THE CRUST IS SOFT, PALE AND SOGGY!

This happens if the oven temperature is too low or the loaf hasn't been fully baked. Check the oven temperature is correct (double check using an oven thermometer) and then return the loaf to the hot oven – set it directly on the oven shelf (rather than in the tin or on a baking sheet) and bake it for a further 5–10 minutes. Always test for 'doneness' by tapping on the underside of a loaf as it will sound hollow when fully baked (see page 29). Brushing with a glaze (as for the Butternut Squash Loaf, page 102) will also help give a good brown crust.

HOW CAN I STOP THE LOAF BECOMING TOO DARK BEFORE IT'S THOROUGHLY BAKED?

Doughs made with sweet ingredients (sugar, honey, maple syrup, dried fruits) and/or finished with an egg-rich glaze can easily catch in the oven as the crust caramelises in the high heat. Keep a beady eye on the bread as it bakes, use an oven thermometer and be ready to rotate the tin or baking sheet so the loaf colours evenly, and cover the top loosely with a sheet of baking paper or foil. For some glazed bakes, such as croissants and brioche, a rich mahogany brown is ideal, and adds to the flavour, so check the recipe.

WHY HAS MY LOAF CRACKED ALONG ONE SIDE?

If the loaf has risen unevenly, or has a crack to one side, it has probably been baked too far to one side of the oven, or too near a hot spot; it's best to check your oven guide for correct shelf position. It's a good idea to rotate the loaf a couple of times during baking so it bakes evenly. Sometimes this happens if you use the wrong tin for baking the dough – if the tin is too small for the quantity of dough it will expand unevenly. The bread will still be perfectly good to eat though.

WHY IS THERE A LARGE TUNNEL OR HOLE IN MY LOAF?

This is a very common problem, even for experienced bakers. It's usually caused by either under-kneading the dough so the gluten is not fully developed, or not baking the loaf enough so the dough in the very centre didn't heat through and set, and on cooling it shrank back leaving a gap. Sometimes a tin loaf (a shaped loaf baked in a tin) has a distinct gap where the dough was rolled up; this is caused by using too much flour on the worktop, which dries the dough. Keep a clean and dry pastry brush at hand for brushing away the excess flour when shaping doughs. If this does happen you can just cut around the hole and still enjoy the rest of your bread.

WHY DOES THE LOAF TASTE YEASTY AND DAMP?

If you use too much yeast, the bread can have an unpleasant aftertaste (it also makes it become stale very quickly) – there's nothing you can do after baking. If the crumb is damp, it wasn't baked for long enough – always test for doneness (see page 29). If the crumb is also very dense this is an indication that the dough wasn't thoroughly kneaded, so the gluten wasn't developed enough to form the structure of the loaf.

BAKE IT BETTER

Recipes

Scones

The key to light scones with a crisp exterior is to work quickly, handling the dough as little as possible and baking in a hot oven. These scones are perfect warm from the oven with jam and clotted cream.

250g self-raising flour
good pinch of salt
50g caster sugar
50g unsalted butter, chilled and diced
1 medium egg

100ml buttermilk, plus extra if needed (or use 2 tablespoons natural yoghurt made up to 100ml with milk)

1. Preheat the oven to 220°C (200°C fan), 425°F, Gas 7 and line a baking sheet with baking paper.

2. Sift the flour, salt and sugar into a mixing bowl. Add the pieces of butter to the bowl and toss them in the flour just to separate and coat them. Rub the butter into the flour using just the tips of your fingers, lifting your hands up above the rim of the bowl so the crumbs and flakes of the mixture fall through your fingers back into the bowl. Keep doing this until the mixture looks like fine crumbs – give the bowl a shake to check there are no lumps of butter visible.

3. Beat the egg with the buttermilk, just until combined, then stir this mixture into the crumbs using a round-bladed knife to make a fairly soft but not wet dough. If there are dry crumbs at the bottom of the bowl, or the dough feels dry and seems difficult to bring together, add a little more buttermilk (or milk) a teaspoon at a time. The dough should look a bit rough and shaggy so don't overwork it and try to keep a light touch.

4. Lightly flour your fingers and the worktop and turn the dough out onto it. **Knead** the dough very gently for just a couple of seconds so it looks slightly smoother, then press the dough out to about 3cm thick.

5. Dip the cutter in some flour (this will make it easier to cut out the scones without them sticking) and stamp out rounds. Gather up the trimmings, press them together and stamp out more rounds.

6. Arrange the rounds on the lined baking sheet, setting them slightly apart to give them space to grow, then dust them lightly with flour. Bake for about 12 minutes, or until a rich golden brown, then transfer to a wire rack to cool slightly. Eat warm from the oven.

Try Something Different

You can easily flavour these scones by stirring the following into the bowl before you add the egg mixture: 50g sultanas or raisins; 50g dried cranberries and the finely grated zest of 1 orange; 50g milk or dark chocolate chips.

HANDS-ON TIME:
10 minutes

BAKING TIME:
12 minutes

MAKES:
8

SPECIAL EQUIPMENT:
baking sheet, 6cm round cutter (plain or fluted)

STORAGE:
Once cold, pop into a freezer bag and freeze for up to 1 month

Drop Scones with Maple Syrup and Lemon

You don't have to heat up the oven to cook these griddle scones – you just need a good, heavy-based frying pan. Also known as Scotch pancakes, they are made from a rich pancake batter sweetened with maple syrup and flavoured with lemon zest – perfect for those mornings when you fancy a change from toast.

HANDS-ON TIME:
5 minutes

COOKING TIME:
4 minutes (cook in batches)

MAKES:
about 16 scones

SPECIAL EQUIPMENT:
flat griddle or heavy-based frying pan

STORAGE:
Wrap in a clean dry cloth and eat the same day or lightly toast the next day

100g plain flour
¾ teaspoon bicarbonate of soda
1½ teaspoons cream of tartar
1 tablespoon caster sugar
finely grated zest of 1 small unwaxed lemon
140ml milk

1 medium egg
2 tablespoons pure maple syrup
a little butter or vegetable oil for the greasing

1. Sift the flour, bicarbonate of soda, cream of tartar and caster sugar into a mixing bowl. Stir in the lemon zest and make a well in the centre of the mixture.

2. Put the milk into a measuring jug, then break in the egg and add the maple syrup. Beat lightly with a fork just until everything is combined. Pour into the well. Using a wire hand whisk, gradually work the flour into the liquids to make a smooth and lump-free batter. Stop whisking as soon as you can't see any lumps as you don't want to overwork the flour and make the scones tough.

3. Heat the griddle or frying pan over a medium heat and grease it very lightly by rubbing it with a dab of soft butter (or splash of oil) on a ball of kitchen paper. Check the pan is the correct heat before you start to cook: drop a teaspoon of the scone batter into the centre of the pan; the batter should hold its shape and the underside turn golden in 2 minutes, so adjust the heat under the pan as necessary.

4. Cook the scones in batches using a tablespoon of batter for each one. Cook for about 2 minutes until the upper surface has started to set, and the underside is golden. Turn the scones over using a palette knife and cook for another 2 minutes until the other side is golden. Transfer the scones to a warm plate lined with a clean dry cloth. Fold over the ends of the cloth to keep the scones warm and eat as soon as possible with butter or a little more maple syrup.

Try Something Different

For a fruitier drop scone, stir in 30g sultanas along with the lemon zest.

Sweet Soda Bread

There's no yeast, no strong bread flour, no kneading and no proving involved here: soda breads are raised and lightened by combining acidic buttermilk and alkaline bicarbonate of soda. This simple yet attractive loaf is full of flavour, although there's plenty of scope for adding extra ingredients (see below for an easy suggestion).

225g stoneground wholemeal plain flour, plus extra for dusting
225g plain white flour
1½ tablespoons light brown muscovado sugar
7g salt
1 teaspoon bicarbonate of soda
375–400ml buttermilk

1. Preheat the oven to 220°C (200°C fan), 425°F, Gas 7. Line a baking sheet with baking paper and lightly dust with flour.

2. Sift both flours, the sugar, salt and bicarbonate of soda into a mixing bowl, then add any specks of bran left in the sieve to the bowl. Make a well in the centre.

3. Pour 375ml of the buttermilk into the well and mix it into the dry ingredients with a round-bladed knife, or your hands, to make a soft and just slightly sticky, rough-looking dough. Different brands of flour vary, so **work** in more buttermilk if the dough feels dry and won't come together.

4. Lightly flour the worktop and your hands, then turn out the dough and quickly shape it into a rough-looking ball. Put the ball onto the prepared baking sheet and gently flatten it so it is about 19cm across and 3cm high.

Sprinkle with a little more wholemeal flour then cut a deep cross in the top – this will help the dough rise and bake evenly as the heat can quickly penetrate the centre. It also gives the loaf the traditional soda bread appearance.

5. Bake for 35–40 minutes, until a deep golden brown. To **test** if the loaf is done, tap it underneath and it should sound hollow. Transfer the loaf to a wire rack and leave to cool until just warm before slicing.

Try Something Different

To make a fruity speckled soda bread, replace the light brown muscovado sugar with 50g demerara sugar, then stir in 150g large raisins or sultanas. Mix and finish the loaf as above but sprinkle with demerara sugar instead of the wholemeal flour. Bake as above.

Easy does it

HANDS-ON TIME:
10 minutes

BAKING TIME:
35–40 minutes

MAKES:
1 medium loaf

SPECIAL EQUIPMENT:
baking sheet

STORAGE:
Once cold, wrap in a clean dry cloth and eat the same day or the next day

Toasted Coconut
Banana Bread

Toasting the unsweetened desiccated coconut deepens the flavour and balances the over-ripe fruit: it's vital to use bananas with skins almost entirely covered with dark brown spots so you know they are ripe enough. Try this spread with lime marmalade for breakfast.

HANDS-ON TIME:
20 minutes

BAKING TIME:
1 hour

MAKES:
1 medium loaf

SPECIAL EQUIPMENT:
450g loaf tin (about 19 × 12.5 × 7.5cm)

STORAGE:
Wrap the cooled loaf tightly in clingfilm or put into a freezer bag and freeze for up to 1 month

50g desiccated coconut
100g unsalted butter, softened
1 medium unwaxed lime
90g light muscovado sugar
2 medium eggs, at room temperature, beaten to mix
250g peeled very ripe bananas (about 3 medium)

3 tablespoons unsweetened natural yoghurt
250g fine wholemeal plain flour
good pinch of salt
1 teaspoon baking powder
½ teaspoon bicarbonate of soda

1. Preheat the oven to 180°C (160°C fan), 350°F, Gas 4. Grease the tin with butter and line the base and two short sides with a long strip of baking paper.

2. Tip the coconut into a baking dish and toast in the oven until it turns a light golden colour – watch carefully as it will only take 3 or 4 minutes. Cool.

3. Meanwhile, put the soft butter into a mixing bowl. Finely grate the lime zest into the bowl then beat with a wooden spoon, or a hand-held electric whisk, until the butter is the consistency of mayonnaise. Add the sugar and beat well until the mixture is fluffy and light.

4. Gradually beat in the eggs, a tablespoon at a time, beating well after each addition – don't worry if the mixture looks slightly sloppy and almost curdled by the time all the eggs have been added; this won't affect the bake.

5. Mash the bananas fairly roughly with a fork – make sure there are some

small lumps so the mixture keeps a bit of texture – then add to the bowl with the toasted coconut. Gently stir in with a large metal spoon or plastic spatula. Squeeze the juice from the lime and add 1 tablespoon to the mixture with the yoghurt then gently stir in.

6. Sift the flour, salt, baking powder and bicarbonate of soda into the bowl (adding any specks of bran left in the sieve) and gently stir in.

7. As soon as everything is thoroughly combined, scrape the mixture into the prepared tin and spread it so the corners are evenly filled and the surface is smooth and flat. Bake for about 1 hour until the top is golden and a cocktail stick or skewer inserted into the centre of the loaf comes out clean.

8. Run a round-bladed knife around the inside of the tin to loosen the loaf then carefully turn it out onto a wire rack. Leave until cold before cutting in thick slices. Best eaten within 3 days.

Very Easy Apple and Cinnamon Buns

These buns are made using the simple technique of stirring wet ingredients into dry – here they are flavoured and topped with chopped apples and baked in paper cases to make the perfect-sized treat for picnics and lunchboxes.

HANDS-ON TIME:
10 minutes

BAKING TIME:
25 minutes

MAKES:
12 buns

SPECIAL EQUIPMENT:
12-hole muffin tin, paper muffin cases

STORAGE:
Best eaten on the day you make them but you can store the cooled buns in an airtight container and eat the next day.

2 large, tart eating apples (about 325–350g in total)
1 tablespoon ground cinnamon
175g plain flour
good pinch of salt
1½ teaspoons baking powder
150g caster sugar

3 medium eggs, at room temperature
3 tablespoons buttermilk
75ml sunflower oil
45g light muscovado sugar
75g pecan pieces
icing sugar, for dusting

1. Preheat the oven to 200°C (180°C fan), 400°F, Gas 6 and fill a 12-hole muffin tin with paper muffin cases.

2. Peel and quarter the apples, then cut out the cores and chop the flesh into chunks roughly the size of your little fingernail – they don't need to be neat or even. Put into a bowl, sprinkle over the cinnamon and toss thoroughly so the chunks are well coated. Put to one side for now.

3. Sift the flour, salt and baking powder into a large mixing bowl, then stir in the caster sugar and make a well in the centre. Put the eggs, buttermilk and sunflower oil in a jug and beat together with a fork until well combined.

4. Pour the egg mixture into the well in the dry ingredients and use a wooden spoon to quickly mix everything together, then add half of the apple/cinnamon mixture and stir well until evenly distributed. The mixture will be very soft and sticky. Save the rest of the apple mix for the topping. Spoon the bun mixture into the tin, dividing it evenly between the muffin cases so that they are about half full.

5. Add the muscovado sugar and pecan pieces to the remaining apple and cinnamon mixture and mix well. Carefully spoon this mixture on top of the buns, making sure they are evenly topped. Bake for 25 minutes, or until the buns feel firm when carefully pressed in the centre. It's a good idea to check after 20 minutes and rotate the tray so they bake evenly.

6. Transfer the buns to a wire rack and leave to cool a little. Dust with icing sugar before serving warm; or enjoy them the next day at room temperature with butter or cream cheese.

Crumpets

The simple yeast batter is boosted with raising agents to give the crumpets their unique holey appearance; they will need to be cooked as soon as the bicarbonate of soda has been added. The dough is mixed – literally – with your hand, which will add warmth to the batter.

225g strong white bread flour
225g plain flour
7g sachet fast-action dried yeast
¾ teaspoon cream of tartar
500ml lukewarm water

6g salt
½ teaspoon bicarbonate of soda
150ml lukewarm milk

Easy does it

HANDS-ON TIME:
30 minutes

HANDS-OFF TIME:
20 minutes + 1 hour

BAKING TIME:
10 minutes

MAKES:
10 crumpets

SPECIAL EQUIPMENT:
heavy-based frying pan or unridged griddle pan, 4 × 9cm crumpet rings (preferably non-stick)

STORAGE:
Once cold, the crumpets can be put into a freezer bag or container and frozen for up to 1 month

1. Put both the flours and the yeast into a large mixing bowl and **mix** thoroughly. Mix in the cream of tartar and make a well in the centre. Pour the lukewarm water into the well, and using your hand gradually beat the flour into the water. Here your hand works like a paddle and is much more efficient than a wooden spoon. Keep beating for about 2 minutes to make a very smooth, thick batter. Cover the bowl tightly with clingfilm and leave on the worktop to **rise** for 1 hour – the batter will increase to about double in size, then sink back.

2. Uncover the bowl and sprinkle the salt over the bubbly batter. Beat the batter with your hand for a minute, then re-cover the bowl and leave for 20 minutes. Lightly grease the crumpet rings with butter.

3. Add the bicarbonate of soda to the lukewarm milk and stir well. Uncover the bowl, pour the milk into the batter and stir gently with a spoon or your hand for a couple of minutes until thoroughly combined. Transfer some of the batter to a jug to make filling the

crumpet rings easier and cover the rest until needed.

4. Set the ungreased griddle or frying pan over a medium heat. When the griddle is very hot, set a crumpet ring just off-centre. Pour in enough batter to half-fill the ring (this will be your 'test' crumpet). If holes do not form on the surface it means the batter is too thick and you will need to stir in a little more lukewarm water; if the batter is too thin and runs out of the ring, stir in a little more flour. As soon as the mixture has puffed up and the surface is set and covered with holes – about 8–9 minutes – very carefully ease off the ring (use a dry tea towel so you don't burn your fingers). Use a palette knife to flip the crumpet over and cook the holey side until lightly speckled – about 2–3 minutes. The flat side should be a deep golden brown so adjust the heat under the griddle as necessary.

5. Wrap the crumpet in a clean tea towel and continue cooking the rest of the batter in batches of three or four. Eat warm from the griddle or toasted, with butter and jam.

Milk and Honey Loaf

Using milk to mix the dough will make the crumb softer and lighter, as well as adding flavour. The result is a slightly domed loaf, with a thin crust, that slices easily for sandwiches and toast, and also keeps well.

500g strong white bread flour, plus extra for dusting
8g fine sea salt
10g unsalted butter, at room temperature, plus a little extra for finishing
7g sachet fast-action dried yeast
10g clear honey
50ml lukewarm water
300ml lukewarm milk

1. Put the flour and salt into a large mixing bowl (or the bowl of a large food mixer fitted with the dough hook attachment) and mix well. Cut the butter into small flakes and add to the bowl. Rub into the flour using just the tips of your fingers, then sprinkle the yeast into the bowl and **mix** in, making sure it is thoroughly combined with the flour. Make a well in the centre.

2. Weigh the honey into a small bowl, add the lukewarm water and stir until dissolved. Pour into the well, followed by the lukewarm milk. Mix everything together with your hands, or use the mixer set on the slowest speed, to make a soft dough. If there are dry crumbs in the base of the bowl, or the dough feels dry and too firm to bring together, add more milk or water a tablespoon at a time. If the dough feels sticky, or clings to the sides of the bowl, then **work** in a little more flour.

3. Sprinkle the worktop with a little flour then turn out the dough. **Knead** the dough thoroughly for 10 minutes, or for 5 minutes using the mixer on the slowest speed, until it feels silky smooth and stretchy. Return the dough to the bowl, if necessary, then cover with a snap-on lid or cling film. Leave to **rise** on the worktop, at normal room temperature, until the ball of dough has doubled in size; this should take about 1 hour. Grease the tin with butter.
Continued

Try Something Different

For a wholemeal loaf replace some or all of the white flour with wholemeal bread flour. You will need to work in a little extra lukewarm milk (or water) to make the dough come together to the right consistency.

Easy does it

HANDS-ON TIME:
30 minutes

HANDS-OFF TIME:
2 hours

BAKING TIME:
35 minutes

MAKES:
1 large loaf

SPECIAL EQUIPMENT:
900g loaf tin (about 26 × 12.5 × 7.5cm)

STORAGE:
Wrap the cooled loaf (whole or sliced) tightly in cling film or put into a freezer bag and freeze for up to 1 month

4. Punch down (**knock back**) the risen dough with your knuckles to deflate it, then turn it out onto a lightly floured worktop. Knead the dough gently for 2 minutes – this is to make sure all the larger air bubbles are deflated and the texture of the dough is very even. Cover the ball of dough with the upturned bowl and leave it to relax for 5 minutes.

5. Lightly flour a rolling pin and roll out the dough to a rectangle about 26 × 30cm and of an even thickness. Starting from one short end roll up the dough fairly tightly (like a Swiss roll), pinching the dough together each time you roll it.

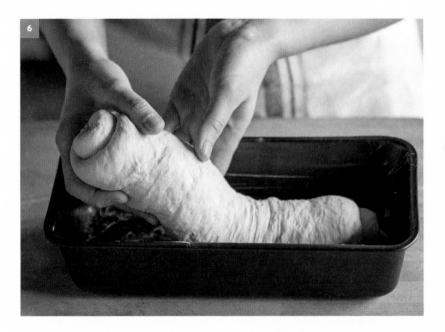

6. Pinch the seam firmly together (for a neater, rounded finish you could tuck the ends under) and set the loaf in the prepared tin, seam-side down. Slip the tin into a large plastic bag, trapping in some air so the plastic doesn't stick to the dough, and tie the ends. Leave the loaf to **prove** and rise on the worktop until it has doubled in size – this will take about 1 hour at normal room temperature. Towards the end of this rising time preheat the oven to 220°C (200°C fan), 425°F, Gas 7.

7. Take the tin out of the bag and bake the loaf for about 35 minutes, or until the top is a rich golden brown. To **test** if the bread is done, carefully turn it out and tap it underneath – if it sounds hollow then the loaf is fully baked, but if there is a dull 'thud' instead, put it back in the tin and bake for a further 5 minutes, then test again.

8. Set the cooked loaf on a wire rack, then rub the top gently with a dab of soft butter on a small ball of kitchen paper – this will give a slightly glossy finish and will help the crust stay soft (if you prefer a crisp crust then omit this step). Leave the bread to cool completely before slicing.

Barm Brack

This round Irish loaf, traditionally baked for Halloween, is more like a spicy cake than simple bread: eat sliced and buttered, or toasted – ghost stories optional. Watch carefully as the loaf bakes as the sweet dough can easily 'catch', leading to an overbrowned crust.

125g currants
125g sultanas
450g strong white bread flour, plus extra for dusting
7g (1½ teaspoons) salt
1 teaspoon mixed spice
1 teaspoon ground cinnamon
few gratings of nutmeg
85g unsalted butter, diced
85g light muscovado sugar
7g sachet fast-action dried yeast
2 medium eggs, at room temperature
125ml lukewarm milk

For the glaze
1 tablespoon caster or granulated sugar

HANDS-ON TIME:
30 minutes, plus soaking

HANDS-OFF TIME:
2–3 hours

BAKING TIME:
50–55 minutes

MAKES:
1 medium loaf

SPECIAL EQUIPMENT:
dough scraper, 20cm round springclip cake tin

STORAGE:
Once cold, wrap (whole or sliced) in clingfilm or use a freezer bag and freeze for up to 1 month

1. Put the currants and sultanas into a medium bowl and add enough hand-hot water to just cover, then leave to soak and slightly soften and plump up just while you make the dough.

2. Put the flour, salt, mixed spice, cinnamon and nutmeg into a large mixing bowl (or the bowl of a free-standing mixer) and **mix** well with your hands. Add the diced butter and rub into the flour, using just the tips of your fingers, until the mixture looks like fine crumbs. Stir in the sugar, then the yeast. Make a well in the centre.

3. Put the eggs and lukewarm milk into a jug and beat lightly with a fork just until combined. Pour into the well then, using your hand as a paddle, gradually **work** the liquid into the flour to make a soft but not sticky dough. If there are dry crumbs in the bottom of the bowl, or if the dough feels dry and hard, work in a little more lukewarm milk, a tablespoon at a time, but make sure that the dough doesn't stick to your fingers or the sides of the bowl. (You can also mix the dough using the dough hook attachment of the mixer on the slowest speed.)

4. Tip the dried fruit mixture into a sieve or colander set over the sink and leave it to drain thoroughly.
Continued

5. Lightly flour the worktop and your fingers and turn out the dough. **Knead** the dough thoroughly for 10 minutes, or 5 minutes with the dough hook on the slowest speed, until the dough feels very smooth and pliable.

6. Scatter the fruit mixture over the dough and very gently knead it into the dough (again, use the slowest speed if using the dough hook). Keep on kneading and turning the dough around until the fruit is evenly distributed: the dough will feel sticky and heavy but try to add as little extra flour as possible (a dough scraper is vital for lifting and turning the dough around on the worktop). Return the dough to the bowl, if necessary, then cover the bowl tightly with cling film or a snap-on lid and leave on the worktop to **rise** for 1–1½ hours, or until doubled in size. Lightly grease the tin with butter.

7. Punch down (**knock back**) the risen dough to deflate it then turn it out onto a lightly floured worktop. Gently **shape** the dough into a ball, then flatten it to make a neat round to fit your tin. Set the round in the prepared tin (make sure it is centred so it bakes to an even shape). Slip the tin into a large plastic bag, trapping in some air so the plastic doesn't stick to the dough, and tie the ends. Leave to **prove** and rise on the worktop for 1–1½ hours, or until the dough has doubled in size. Towards the end of the rising time preheat the oven to 200°C (180°C fan), 400°F, Gas 6.

8. Uncover the tin and bake the loaf for about 50–55 minutes, or until it is a rich brown and the turned-out loaf sounds hollow when tapped underneath. It's a good idea to **test** the loaf after 40 minutes and cover the top with a sheet of baking paper or foil, if it seems to be browning too quickly.

9. Set the baked loaf back in its tin, then quickly make the sticky glaze by dissolving the sugar in 2 tablespoons boiling water from the kettle. Brush this glaze over the top of the loaf then put it back into the oven for another 2 minutes. Turn the loaf out onto a wire rack and leave to cool completely before slicing.

Try Something Different

To make an iced loaf, omit the sticky glaze and instead mix 6 tablespoons fondant icing sugar with 1½–2 teaspoons cold water to make a thick smooth paste, then spoon or spread over the top of the cold loaf and leave until set before slicing.

Bara Brith

Otherwise known as Welsh Currant Bread, this is perfect thickly sliced and spread with slightly salted butter, or tangy soft cheese. Soaking the dried fruit makes the dough softer than usual, so knead it gently in the mixing bowl. Watch carefully during baking to avoid over-browning.

225g dried mixed fruit (currants, raisins, sultanas and chopped peel)
350ml strong hot tea
60g light muscovado sugar
½ teaspoon mixed spice

50g unsalted butter, melted
475g strong white bread flour, plus extra for dusting
7g (1½ teaspoons) salt
7g sachet fast-action dried yeast

1. Put the dried fruit in a heatproof bowl and stir in the hot tea. Cover and leave to soak for at least 6 hours, or overnight. The next day stir in the sugar, mixed spice and melted butter.

2. In a separate, larger bowl combine the flour and salt then **mix** in the yeast with your hand. Add the wet fruit mixture to the bowl and **work** everything together to make a very soft, slightly sticky, dough – if the dough feels stiff or dry, work in a little lukewarm water, a tablespoon at a time.

3. Gently **knead** the dough in the bowl for 5 minutes or until the fruit is evenly distributed and the dough feels very elastic, pliable and lighter. Cover the bowl with clingfilm and leave the dough to **rise** on the worktop for 1½–2 hours at room temperature, or until doubled in size. Grease the tin with butter.

4. Punch down (**knock back**) the risen dough to deflate it, then lightly flour the worktop and your fingers and turn the dough out. **Shape** the dough into a loaf to fit the tin: gently pat it out to an even 26 × 30cm rectangle, then roll

it up fairly tightly from one short end, like a Swiss roll, pinching the dough together as you go. Pinch the seam to seal the roll then tuck under the ends and gently lift the loaf into the prepared tin, seam-side down.

5. Slip the tin into a large plastic bag, trapping in some air so the plastic doesn't stick to the dough, and tie the ends. Leave the dough to **prove** and rise on the worktop for 1½–2 hours, until it has doubled in size. Towards the end of the rising time, preheat the oven to 200°C (180°C fan), 400°F, Gas 6.

6. Remove the tin from the bag and bake for 30 minutes, checking after 25 minutes: if necessary rotate the tin so it colours evenly. If it looks like it is browning too much cover the top with a sheet of baking paper or foil. After another 5 minutes, **test** for 'doneness' by turning out the loaf and tapping the base: if it sounds hollow, the loaf is baked, if not return the loaf to the tin and bake for another 5 minutes, then test again. Turn the baked loaf out onto a wire rack and leave to cool completely before slicing.

HANDS-ON TIME:
25 minutes

HANDS-OFF TIME:
6 hours or overnight
+ 3–4 hours

BAKING TIME:
30–35 minutes

MAKES:
1 large loaf

SPECIAL EQUIPMENT:
900g loaf tin (about 26 × 12.5 × 7.5cm)

STORAGE:
Once cold, wrap in clingfilm (whole or sliced) or pop into freezer bags and freeze for up to 1 month

Apricot and Macadamia Light Rye Loaf

Using a small proportion of rye flour boosts the flavour of a dough without making it difficult to work or heavy to eat. This good-looking bread slices well and is an ideal accompaniment to pâtés, terrines and cheeses, as well as breakfast toast.

100g soft-dried apricots
1 tablespoon clear honey
175ml boiling water
75g macadamia nuts
450g strong white bread flour
50g wholemeal rye flour, plus extra for dusting
8g salt
7g sachet fast-action dried yeast
175ml lukewarm milk

1. Preheat the oven to 180°C (160°C fan), 350°F, Gas 4 and line a baking sheet with baking paper.

2. Using kitchen scissors snip the apricots into quarters and put them into a heatproof bowl. Add the honey and boiling water then leave until the water cools to lukewarm, by which time the fruit will have plumped up. Meanwhile, tip the macadamia nuts into a baking dish and put in the oven until lightly toasted, about 5 minutes. Set to one side to cool until needed.

3. Put both the flours and salt into a large mixing bowl, or the bowl of a free-standing mixer, and **mix** well. Sprinkle the yeast into the bowl and thoroughly mix in. Stir in the cooled nuts and then make a well in the centre.

4. Dip your finger into the apricot soaking water to check it is lukewarm, then tip the apricots and the liquid into the well. Pour in the lukewarm milk and gradually **work** the liquid into the flour, using your hand or the dough hook attachment of the mixer set to its slowest speed. You are looking for a soft but not sticky dough; flours vary so if there are dry crumbs in the base of the bowl, or the dough feels dry or hard, work in a little more lukewarm water, a tablespoon at a time.
Continued

Try Something Different

For a different fruit and nut combination, use the same amount of soft-dried figs and hazelnuts instead of the apricots and macadamia nuts.

Easy does it

HANDS-ON TIME:
30 minutes

HANDS-OFF TIME:
2–2½ hours

BAKING TIME:
35 minutes

MAKES:
1 large loaf

SPECIAL EQUIPMENT:
baking sheet

STORAGE:
Once cold, tightly wrap the loaf (whole or sliced) in clingfilm or put into a freezer bag and freeze for up to 1 month

5. Dust the worktop with a little rye flour, then turn out the dough and **knead** it thoroughly for 10 minutes (or 5 minutes with the dough hook on slow speed), or until it feels very elastic and slightly firmer. Don't worry if the nuts break up a little during kneading. Return the dough to the bowl, if necessary, then cover tightly with clingfilm or a snap-on lid and leave to **rise** on the worktop until doubled in size – about 1–1½ hours.

6. Punch down (**knock back**) the risen dough to deflate it, then turn it out onto the worktop (again, lightly sprinkled with rye flour). Gently knead the dough for 1 minute then **shape** into an oval about 23cm long. Make a good crease lengthwise along the centre of the dough using the edge of your hand, then roll the dough over to make a neat sausage shape (with the crease in the centre of the dough).

7. Gently roll the dough onto the lined baking sheet so the seam is underneath, then use your hands to shape the loaf into a neat and even oval. Sprinkle the top with a little more rye flour then slip the baking sheet into a large plastic bag, trapping in some air so the plastic doesn't stick to the dough. Leave to **prove** and rise on the worktop until doubled in size – about 1 hour. Towards the end of the rising time preheat the oven to 220°C (200°C fan), 425°F, Gas 7.

8. Uncover the risen loaf and, using a large sharp knife or razor blade, make 5 slashes across the top on a slight diagonal. Bake for 30–35 minutes, or until the loaf is a good golden brown. **Test** the bread is cooked by tapping the base – it should sound hollow. If there's a dull 'thud', pop the loaf back in the oven for another 5 minutes, then test again. Turn the cooked loaf out onto a wire rack and leave to cool completely before slicing.

Traditional
Hot Cross Buns

Rich with spices and studded with vine fruits and chopped mixed peel, the buns are finished with a piped dough cross before baking and glazed after baking for a brilliant shine.

350g strong white bread flour, plus extra for dusting
100g wholegrain bread flour (wheat or spelt)
7g salt
3 tablespoons caster sugar
2 teaspoons mixed spice
7g sachet fast-action dried yeast
50g unsalted butter, at room temperature, diced
125g dried mixed fruit and peel
2 medium eggs, at room temperature
175ml lukewarm milk

For the piped cross
4 tablespoons strong white bread flour
about 2 tablespoons cold water

For the glaze
4 tablespoons very hot milk
2 tablespoons caster sugar

Easy does it

HANDS-ON TIME:
30 minutes

HANDS-OFF TIME:
1¾ hours

BAKING TIME:
15 minutes

MAKES:
12 buns

SPECIAL EQUIPMENT:
baking sheet, small disposable piping bag

STORAGE:
Once cold, the buns can be packed into a freezer bag and frozen for up to 1 month

1. Combine both the flours, salt, sugar and mixed spice in a large mixing bowl or the bowl of a free-standing mixer. Sprinkle the yeast into the bowl and **mix** in. When thoroughly combined add the pieces of butter and rub into the flour mixture using just the tips of your fingers. When the mixture looks like fine crumbs mix in the dried fruit mixture. Make a well in the centre.

2. Add the eggs to the lukewarm milk and beat with a fork until thoroughly combined, then pour into the well in the flour mixture. Using your hand, or the dough hook attachment of the mixer on slow speed, gradually **work** the liquid into the flour to make a soft but not sticky dough. Flours vary so if there are dry crumbs in the base of the bowl, or if the dough feels stiff and dry, work in more milk, a tablespoon at a time. If the dough sticks to the sides of the bowl, work in more flour, a tablespoon at a time.

3. Lightly flour the worktop and your fingers then turn out the dough and **knead** it thoroughly for 10 minutes or until it feels very elastic and silky smooth – try to use as little extra flour as possible for kneading as it can make the dough too dry. (You can also knead the dough for about 5 minutes using the dough hook on slow speed.)

4. Return the dough to the bowl, if necessary, then cover it tightly with clingfilm or a snap-on lid. Leave to **rise** on the worktop until doubled in size – about 1 hour. Line a baking sheet with baking paper.
Continued

5. Uncover the risen dough and punch down (**knock back**) to deflate it. Weigh the deflated dough and divide it into 12 equal portions. Using your hands, **shape** each portion of dough into a neat ball then arrange them 3cm apart on the lined baking sheet. Slip the baking sheet into a large plastic bag, trapping in some air so the plastic doesn't stick to the dough, and tie the ends. Leave to **prove** and rise on the worktop until doubled in size – about 45 minutes. Towards the end of the rising time preheat the oven to 200°C (180°C fan), 400°F, Gas 6.

6. To make the piped cross, put the 4 tablespoons strong white bread flour into a small bowl and stir in about 2 tablespoons of cold water to make a smooth, thick mixture that can be piped (you may not need all the water). Spoon into a disposable piping bag and snip off the tip. Uncover the buns and pipe a cross over the top of each one.

7. Bake the buns for 15 minutes, or until they are a good golden brown. Set the baking sheet on a wire rack while you glaze the buns: mix the 4 tablespoons very hot (just below boiling point) milk with the 2 tablespoons caster sugar, just until the sugar has dissolved, then quickly brush the hot, sticky glaze over the hot buns. Transfer the buns to a wire rack and leave to cool.

Try Something Different

For a different flavour use a bag of luxury dried fruit mix (containing glacé cherries and chopped apricots) or use a mixture of soft-dried cherries and berries.

Muesli Round with Rhubarb and Strawberry Compote

Oat-based Swiss Bircher-style muesli, soaked in apple juice, adds plenty of texture as well as flavour to a bread dough. The dough will feel slightly 'gluey' or gummy thanks to the oats, but will bake to a craggy, chewy, moist loaf that's delicious for breakfast, especially when served with this fresh fruit compote.

250g Swiss Bircher muesli
400ml cloudy apple juice, at room temperature
125g strong white bread flour, plus extra for dusting
125g wholegrain spelt bread flour
8g salt
7g sachet fast-action dried yeast
extra muesli (or spelt flour), for sprinkling

For the rhubarb and strawberry compote
400g pink rhubarb, trimmed and cut into 2cm chunks
250g strawberries, hulled and halved if very large
3 tablespoons clear honey, or to taste

Easy does it

HANDS-ON TIME:
25 minutes

HANDS-OFF TIME:
2–5 hours + 2 hours

BAKING TIME:
35 minutes

MAKES:
1 large loaf

SPECIAL EQUIPMENT:
baking sheet

STORAGE:
Once cold, wrap (whole or sliced) in clingfilm or pop into a freezer bag and freeze for up to 1 month

1. Tip the muesli into a mixing bowl and stir in the apple juice. Cover and leave to soak for at least 2 hours, but no more than 5 hours.

2. Meanwhile, prepare the compote. Put the rhubarb chunks and strawberries into a medium pan and add the honey. Place over a very low heat and cook gently, stirring occasionally, for 8–10 minutes, or until the rhubarb is just tender when pierced with the tip of a sharp knife. Taste and add more honey as needed. Allow to cool and then chill until needed.

3. Put both the flours and the salt into a large bowl, or the bowl of a free-standing mixer, and mix well. Sprinkle in the yeast and **mix** in.

4. Scrape the soaked mixture into the large bowl then mix everything together with your hand, or the dough hook attachment on slow speed, to make a soft dough that feels slightly 'gummy'. Mueslis and flours vary so if the dough feels dry and crumbly, or is difficult to bring together, **work** in more apple juice (or water), a teaspoon at a time.

5. Leave the mixed dough to sit in the bowl for 5 minutes to let the flours become fully **hydrated** before you start to knead. At this point, if the dough seems stiff, work in a little more apple juice or water.
Continued

6. Sprinkle the worktop and your fingers with a little flour then turn out the dough and **knead** it thoroughly for 10 minutes (or 5 minutes with the dough hook on the slowest speed) until the dough feels stretchy and pliable.

7. Return the dough to the bowl, if necessary, then cover it tightly with clingfilm or a snap-on lid and leave to **rise** on the worktop until doubled in size – about 1 hour. Line a baking sheet with baking paper.

8. Punch down (**knock back**) the risen dough to deflate it, then turn it out onto a lightly floured worktop. Gently knead the dough for a couple of seconds just to **shape** it into a neat ball about 18cm across.

9. Transfer the dough to the lined baking sheet and sprinkle the loaf with a little muesli (or spelt flour).

10. Using a very sharp knife, or razor blade, slash the top several times vertically then horizontally to make a neat chequerboard pattern (the top will crack as it rises and then again in the heat of the oven, so this will help keep the loaf in shape).

11. Slip the sheet into a large plastic bag, trapping in some air so the plastic doesn't stick to the dough, and tie the ends. Leave on the worktop to **prove** and rise until the loaf has doubled in size – about 1 hour. Towards the end of the rising time, preheat the oven to 220°C (200°C fan), 425°F, Gas 7.

12. Uncover the loaf and bake for about 35 minutes, or until golden brown. To **test** if the loaf is cooked, tap the base of the loaf: it should sound hollow. Transfer to a wire rack and leave to cool completely before slicing. Serve with the rhubarb and strawberry compote.

Try Something Different

The same dough can be shaped into 12 triangular rolls. At the end of Step 7 gently flatten the ball to make a 25cm round, then cut into 12 wedges. Gently pull the wedges apart and transfer to the baking sheet. Sprinkle with muesli then leave to rise as above and bake for about 20 minutes.

Yorkshire Teacakes

Large and fairly flat, these buns, studded with dried sultanas, raisins and currants, are made to be split then toasted and eaten hot with butter at teatime. Shaping is key here, so take the time to divide the dough evenly and roll and flatten into neat discs.

450g strong white bread flour, plus extra for dusting
6g salt
2 tablespoons caster sugar
7g sachet fast-action dried yeast
50g unsalted butter, at room temperature

100g dried mixed vine fruit (sultanas, raisins, currants)
250ml lukewarm milk
extra milk, for brushing

HANDS-ON TIME:
30 minutes

HANDS-OFF TIME:
1¾–2 hours

BAKING TIME:
20 minutes

MAKES:
8 teacakes

SPECIAL EQUIPMENT:
2 baking sheets

STORAGE:
Once cold, put whole or split teacakes into freezer bags and freeze for up to 1 month (split teacakes can be toasted from frozen)

1. Put the flour, salt and sugar in a large mixing bowl, or the bowl of a free-standing mixer, and **mix** well. Sprinkle in the yeast and mix thoroughly. Add the diced butter and rub into the flour, using the tips of your fingers, until the mixture looks like fine crumbs. Add the dried fruit and mix in, breaking up any clumps. Make a well in the centre.

2. Pour the lukewarm milk into the well, then gradually **work** everything together using your hand, or the dough hook attachment on the slowest speed, to make a soft but not sticky dough. If the dough feels dry or difficult to bring together, work in more milk, a tablespoon at a time. If the dough sticks to your fingers or the bowl, work in a little more flour, a tablespoon at a time.

3. Turn the dough onto a lightly floured worktop and **knead** until very pliable and stretchy – about 10 minutes, or 5 minutes using the dough hook on the slowest speed. Return the dough to the bowl, if necessary, then tightly cover the bowl with clingfilm or a snap-on lid. Leave on the worktop to **rise** for about 1 hour, or until doubled in size. Line 2 baking sheets with baking paper.

4. Punch down (**knock back**) the risen dough to deflate it, then turn it out onto a lightly floured worktop. Dust your fingers with flour and knead the dough briefly just to shape it into a ball. Weigh and divide the dough into 8 equal portions. **Shape** each portion into a neat ball. Cover with a dry tea towel and leave to rest for 5 minutes.

5. Gently flatten the balls with your fingers to make 8 perfectly round discs 10cm across and about 2cm high. Space them well apart on the lined baking sheets, and cover loosely with clingfilm. Leave to **prove** and rise on the worktop for 45–60 minutes, or until doubled in size. Towards the end of the rising time preheat the oven to 200°C (180°C fan), 400°F, Gas 6.

6. Glaze the risen teacakes with extra milk – to give them a good, rich shine. Bake for 18–20 minutes, or until a deep golden colour. Transfer to a wire rack to cool completely before splitting in half.

Iced Fingers

Very soft and light, these slightly sweet bread fingers are filled with red jam and topped with a slick of coloured icing – an ever-popular old-fashioned treat, sometimes called London buns. The dough needs to be slightly soft, but firm enough to hold a good shape. Try to keep the icing as neat as you can!

450g strong white bread flour, plus extra for dusting
6g salt
45g caster sugar
50g unsalted butter, chilled and diced
7g sachet fast-action dried yeast
1 medium egg, at room temperature
225ml lukewarm milk

To finish
4 tablespoons seedless or sieved raspberry jam
250g fondant icing sugar
pink and yellow food colouring pastes

1. Put the flour, salt and sugar into a large bowl, or the bowl of a free-standing mixer, and **mix** well with your hand or the dough hook attachment. Add the diced butter to the bowl and rub it into the flour, using just the tips of your fingers, until the mixture looks like fine crumbs. Sprinkle the yeast on top and thoroughly mix in. Make a well in the centre.

2. Add the egg to the lukewarm milk and beat with a fork, just until combined, then pour into the well. Using your hand, or the dough hook attachment on slow speed, gradually **work** the liquid into the flour to make a soft but not sticky dough. If the dough feels stiff and dry, or there are dry crumbs in the base of the bowl, work in more lukewarm milk, a tablespoon at a time. If the dough sticks to the sides of the bowl or won't hold a shape, work in more flour, a tablespoon at a time.

3. Turn out the dough onto a lightly floured worktop and **knead** it thoroughly for 10 minutes, or 5 minutes using the dough hook on slow speed, until it feels slightly firmer and very smooth and elastic. Return the dough to the bowl, if necessary, and cover it tightly with clingfilm or a snap-on lid. Leave to **rise** on the worktop for about 1 hour, or until doubled in size. Line a baking sheet with baking paper.
Continued

Easy does it

HANDS-ON TIME:
50 minutes

HANDS-OFF TIME:
1¾ hours

BAKING TIME:
12 minutes

MAKES:
12 fingers

SPECIAL EQUIPMENT:
baking sheet, squeezy icing bottle or small piping bag fitted with a 2–3mm plain round piping nozzle

STORAGE:
Best eaten the day they are made

4. Punch down (**knock back**) the risen dough to deflate it, then turn it out onto a very lightly floured worktop and knead it briefly, just to shape it into a ball. Weigh the dough and divide it into 12 equal portions. **Shape** each portion into a neat ball then, with your hands, roll it on the worktop into a perfectly even sausage or finger 12cm long.

5. Set the fingers 2.5cm apart on the lined baking sheet then cover very loosely with a large sheet of clingfilm (or slip the sheet into a large plastic bag, trapping some air inside to stop the plastic sticking to the dough, and tie the ends). Leave on the worktop to **prove** and rise for about 45 minutes, or until the fingers have doubled in size and are just touching. Towards the end of the rising time preheat the oven to 220°C (200°C fan), 425°F, Gas 7.

6. Uncover the fingers and bake for 12–15 minutes, or until golden brown – check after 10 minutes and rotate the baking sheet so the fingers colour evenly. Remove and transfer to a wire rack to cool completely.

Try Something Different

To make orange cardamom fingers, add the finely grated zest of 1 medium orange and the crushed seeds of 4 cardamom pods to the flour with the sugar, then make and bake as the main recipe. Cool, then split horizontally and fill with lemon (or orange) curd – about 150g. Whip 200ml chilled double cream with ½ teaspoon vanilla extract and 2 teaspoons icing sugar to soft peaks. Transfer to a piping bag fitted with a 1cm plain round nozzle and pipe a line or dots of cream on top of the curd. Make up the fondant icing using squeezed orange juice instead of water and ice the top of each finger. Leave plain or decorate with shreds of orange peel and leave to set.

7. To finish the fingers, stir the 4 tablespoons of raspberry jam well so it is fluid, then transfer to a squeezy bottle or a piping bag fitted with a 2–3mm plain round piping nozzle. Carefully pull the fingers apart. Push the tip of the bottle into the middle of one long side of one finger and squeeze in a little jam – about a teaspoon. Repeat with the other fingers.

8. Sift the 250g fondant icing sugar into a bowl and gradually stir in about 3 tablespoons cold water, or enough to make a smooth and thick icing that just runs off the back of the spoon. Divide the icing between three shallow bowls. Leave one bowl of icing white and use a cocktail stick to add pink and yellow food colouring paste to each of the

other bowls. Always add the colour a little at a time, mixing well until the icing is the shade you want.

9. Dip the fingers into the icing, one at a time, smoothing off the excess with your finger. (Alternatively, if you find this step a bit sticky and messy, you can spoon the icing over the top of each finger.) Leave to set on a wire rack until the icing is firm, about 45 minutes, before serving.

Devonshire Splits

These little buns have a very soft and light crumb and a thin, sweet crust. The texture of the dough is crucial – it should be soft but still hold its shape, and be perfectly kneaded. If your kitchen is cool it is a good idea to warm the mixing bowl before mixing the dough as the gentle heat will help create a light dough.

400g strong white bread flour, plus extra for dusting
6g salt
1 teaspoon sugar
60g unsalted butter, at room temperature, diced
7g sachet fast-action dried yeast
250ml lukewarm milk
vegetable oil for greasing
icing sugar, for dusting

To serve
225g clotted cream
300g raspberry jam

Easy does it

HANDS-ON TIME:
35 minutes

HANDS-OFF TIME:
1 hour 50 minutes

BAKING TIME:
15 minutes

MAKES:
12 buns

SPECIAL EQUIPMENT:
large baking sheet

STORAGE:
Leave the unsplit and unfilled buns to cool completely, then pop into a freezer bag and freeze for up to 1 month

1. Put the flour, salt and sugar into a mixing bowl, or the bowl of a free-standing mixer, and **mix** well with your hand. Add the pieces of butter and rub in with the tips of your fingers until the mixture looks like fine crumbs. Sprinkle the yeast into the bowl and thoroughly mix in. Then make a well in the centre.

2. Pour the lukewarm milk into the bowl and using your hand, or the dough hook attachment of the mixer on slow speed, gradually **work** the liquid into the flour mixture to make a soft, but not too sticky dough. If the dough feels dry or crumbly, and is hard to bring together, work in more lukewarm milk, a tablespoon at a time. If the dough sticks to your fingers or the sides of the bowl, work in a little more flour.

3. Before you start kneading rub a little oil over the worktop, instead of sprinkling it with flour (the dough will firm up as you knead it and you want to avoid working in extra flour and making the dough tough and dry). Scrape out the dough and **knead** it thoroughly until it feels very pliable and satiny smooth – about 10 minutes (or 5 minutes with the dough hook on slow speed). Return the dough to the bowl, if necessary, and cover it tightly with clingfilm or a snap-on lid and leave it to **rise** on the worktop for about 1 hour, or until doubled in size.

4. Punch down (**knock back**) the risen dough to deflate it then turn it out onto a worktop very lightly dusted with flour. Knead it once or twice to bring it into a ball then weigh the dough and divide it into 12 equal portions. Cover the portions of dough with a dry tea towel and leave to rest for 5 minutes before shaping.
Continued

5. To **shape** the round buns, form one portion of dough into a ball on the worktop then cup your hand over the ball (you want to have your fingertips and wrist just touching the worktop) and gently rotate your hand so the dough rolls around, smoothing the surface and shaping it into a neat ball.

6. Line a large baking sheet with baking paper and arrange the rolls on it in four rows of three, setting them 2cm apart. Slip the sheet into a large plastic bag, trapping in some air so the plastic doesn't stick to the dough, and tie the ends. Leave to **prove** and rise on the worktop until the buns have doubled in size, about 45 minutes. Towards the end of the rising time preheat the oven to 220°C (200°C fan), 425°F, Gas 7.

7. Uncover the buns – they will now be touching – and bake for 15–18 minutes, or until the buns are a rich golden colour; check after 13 minutes and rotate the sheet so the buns colour evenly.

8. As soon as the buns are ready, set the sheet on a wire rack and quickly sift icing sugar over the top. Carefully slide the buns, still on the baking paper, onto the rack and cover with a dry tea towel – this will keep the crust soft. Leave for a few minutes, until barely warm.

9. Uncover and gently pull the buns apart. (To freeze the buns, leave them to cool completely.) While they are still warm, carefully split them horizontally and fill with the clotted cream and raspberry jam. Dust with more icing sugar and serve immediately.

Sticky Malted Loaf

The sweet, sticky malt extract gives this loaf its unique, caramelly flavour. The best way to incorporate such a thick syrup is to use the quick melt-and-mix method, where all the ingredients go into a large pan – no kneading and no rising.

Easy does it

HANDS-ON TIME:
15 minutes

BAKING TIME:
50 minutes

MAKES:
1 medium loaf

SPECIAL
EQUIPMENT:
900g loaf tin (about
26 × 12.5 × 7.5cm)

STORAGE:
Once cold, wrap in
foil and store in an
airtight container
or cake tin for up to
5 days

80g malt extract
1 tablespoon golden syrup
25g dark muscovado sugar
150ml water
25g unsalted butter
300g stoned chopped dates
½ teaspoon bicarbonate of soda
100g walnut pieces

1 medium egg, at room temperature, lightly beaten
225g wholemeal plain flour
2 teaspoons baking powder
good pinch of salt

1. Weigh the malt extract into a pan large enough to hold all the ingredients (warm a metal spoon in hot water first so that the malt extract slides from the spoon). Add the golden syrup, sugar, water, butter and dates. Set the pan over a low heat, stirring with a wooden spoon until the butter melts.

2. Bring to a boil then simmer for a minute, stirring. Remove the pan from the heat and stir in the bicarbonate of soda – the mixture will foam up. When thoroughly combined leave to cool until the mixture feels lukewarm when you dip in your little finger. Meanwhile, preheat the oven to 170°C (150°C fan), 325°F, Gas 3 and grease the inside and the rim of the tin with butter. Line it with a long strip of baking paper to cover the base and two short sides.

3. Add the walnuts and beaten egg to the pan and mix in thoroughly. Sift the flour, baking powder and salt into the pan (add any specks of bran left in the sieve to the pan) and stir everything together until thoroughly combined.

4. Scrape the heavy, sticky mixture into the tin and spread it evenly so the corners are equally filled and the surface is flat and smooth. Bake for about 45 minutes, or until golden brown and a skewer inserted into the centre comes out clean; check the bread after 40 minutes to avoid over-baking.

5. Remove the tin from the oven and set it on a wire rack. Run a round-bladed knife around the inside to loosen the loaf, then leave it to cool completely before removing from the tin. Peel off the lining paper, then wrap in foil. Leave for 24 hours to allow the flavours to develop and deepen before cutting into thick slices and spreading with butter.

Try Something Different

For a sweeter, softer texture replace the walnut pieces with the same quantity of raisins.

Cinnamon and Raisin Bagels

The famous chewy crumb and glossy crust is the result of quickly poaching the risen dough rings in boiling water before baking. There is a big difference between 'chewy' and 'tough', so do follow all the resting times for the dough.

Easy does it

HANDS-ON TIME:
50 minutes

HANDS-OFF TIME:
1 hour 50 minutes

BAKING TIME:
20 minutes

MAKES:
12 bagels

SPECIAL
EQUIPMENT:
2 or 3 baking sheets

STORAGE:
Once cold, wrap
the bagels (whole
or split) in clingfilm
or pop into a freezer
bag and freeze for up
to 1 month

500g extra-strong white bread flour, plus extra for dusting
2 teaspoons ground cinnamon
8g salt
30g light muscovado sugar
7g sachet fast-action dried yeast
50g raisins
250ml lukewarm water
1 medium egg, at room temperature
2 teaspoons malt extract
2 tablespoons sunflower oil or melted butter

To finish
1 tablespoon malt extract, for poaching
1 medium egg white plus a pinch of salt, to glaze

1. Put the flour, cinnamon, salt and sugar into a large mixing bowl, or the bowl of a free-standing mixer, and **mix** well with your hand. Sprinkle in the yeast, mix in, then add the raisins and mix thoroughly. Make a well in the centre.

2. Put the lukewarm water into a jug, break in the egg and add the malt extract and sunflower oil (or melted butter). Beat everything together with a fork until combined. Pour the liquid mixture into the well in the flour then with your hand, or the dough hook on the slowest speed, gradually draw in the flour to make a soft but not sticky dough. If the dough feels tough or dry, or if there are dry crumbs in the base of the bowl, **work** in more water, a tablespoon at a time. Cover the bowl with clingfilm, a snap-on lid or a damp tea towel and leave it to rest for 10 minutes – this makes kneading this dough easier.

3. Turn out the dough onto a lightly floured worktop and **knead** it very thoroughly for 10 minutes, or 5 minutes using the dough hook on the slowest speed, until the dough feels very elastic and smooth. Return the dough to the bowl, if necessary, and cover with clingfilm or a snap-on lid, or slip the bowl into a large plastic bag and close the ends tightly. Leave to **rise** on the worktop at room temperature for 1½ hours, or until doubled in size.

4. Punch down (**knock back**) the risen dough with your knuckles to deflate it, then turn it out onto a lightly floured work surface. Knead the dough once or twice just to shape it into a ball then weigh it and divide it into 12 equal portions. **Shape** each piece of dough into a neat ball, then cover with a dry tea towel and leave the dough to relax for 10 minutes.
Continued

5. Slightly flatten the balls with your hands, then push a floured forefinger through the centre of each ball to form a ring.

6. Gently twirl and rotate the ring on your finger to enlarge the hole by stretching the dough; it will close up a little as it cooks so aim to make the hole about 3cm across now. Arrange the bagels, spaced well apart, on a well-floured baking sheet. Cover once more with the dry tea towel and leave for 15 minutes. Meanwhile, preheat the oven to 200°C (180°C fan), 400°F, Gas 6 and line two baking sheets with baking paper.

7. Bring a large pan of water to the boil and stir in the 1 tablespoon of malt extract (this will help give a nice shiny crust). Gently drop the bagels, two or three at a time, into the boiling water and poach for exactly 30 seconds – they will swell up so avoid overcrowding the pan. Using a slotted spoon, carefully flip them over and poach for a further 30 seconds. Lift out the bagels with the slotted spoon, draining them thoroughly, and arrange them on the lined baking sheets, spaced well apart.

8. When all the bagels have been poached beat the 1 egg white with a pinch of salt just until broken up, then very lightly brush it over the bagels to glaze. Don't get the glaze on the baking paper as this will 'glue' the dough to it. Bake for about 20 minutes until they are a glossy golden brown. Remove from the oven and put them on a wire rack to cool completely before splitting and eating. Best eaten the same day, or toasted the next day.

Try Something Different

For a cinnamon and choc chip version, simply replace the raisins with the same amount of dark chocolate chips and continue as above.

Cornish Saffron Buns

The dough is coloured and richly flavoured with saffron, which has been toasted and then soaked for maximum impact. The butter is incorporated fairly easily – by rubbing it into the flour – to make a lovely soft dough that is easy to handle and bakes to a soft, moist crumb and crust. A rich dough like this one will take longer to rise than a plain dough, so be patient.

Easy does it

HANDS-ON TIME:
35 minutes

HANDS-OFF TIME:
4½–5½ hours +
1–12 hours to soak
the saffron

BAKING TIME:
20 minutes

MAKES:
16 buns

SPECIAL
EQUIPMENT:
2 baking sheets

STORAGE:
Once cold, pack
into a freezer bag or
airtight container
and freeze for up to
1 month

1 teaspoon saffron strands
3 tablespoons lukewarm water
500g strong white bread flour, plus extra for dusting
8g salt
75g caster sugar
175g unsalted butter, chilled and diced
7g sachet fast-action dried yeast
225g dried mixed vine fruit and chopped peel
175ml lukewarm semi-skimmed milk

To finish
25g unsalted butter, melted
2 tablespoons demerara sugar

1. Preheat the oven to 180°C (160°C fan), 350°F, Gas 4. Crumble the saffron into a ramekin and toast in the oven for about 10 minutes until the strands turn a darker red. (You can turn off the oven for now.) Add the lukewarm water, cover and leave to soak for at least 1 hour or for up to 12 hours.

2. When you are ready to make up the dough, put the flour, salt and sugar into a large mixing bowl, or the bowl of a free-standing mixer, and **mix** thoroughly with your hand. Add the diced butter to the bowl and rub it in using the tips of your fingers until the mixture looks like fine crumbs. Add the yeast and the dried fruit mixture, and mix well, breaking up any clumps of fruit. Make a well in the centre.

Continued

3. Pour the soaked saffron strands and liquid into the well, followed by the 175ml lukewarm milk. Using your hand, or the dough hook attachment of the mixer on slow speed, gradually **work** the liquid into the flour mixture to make a soft but not sticky dough. If the dough feels dry or stiff (or there are dry crumbs at the base of the bowl) work in more milk or water, a tablespoon at a time. If the dough clings to your fingers, or the sides of the bowl, work in more flour, a little at a time. The dough will firm up during kneading so it shouldn't feel too firm at this point.

4. Turn out the dough onto a lightly floured worktop and **knead** thoroughly until it feels very silky, pliable and elastic – about 10 minutes, or 5 minutes using the dough hook on slow speed. Return the dough to the bowl, if necessary, and cover it tightly with clingfilm or a snap-on lid and leave to **rise** in a gently warm (not hot) spot for 2½–3 hours, or until doubled in size. Line two baking sheets with baking paper.

5. Punch down (**knock back**) the risen dough to deflate it then turn it out onto a very lightly floured worktop. Knead it once or twice to form a ball then weigh the dough and divide it into 16 equal portions. **Shape** each into a neat ball then cup your hand over the ball (you want to have your fingertips and wrist just touching the worktop) and gently rotate your hand so the dough rolls around, smoothing the surface and shaping it into a neat ball.

6. Arrange the buns well apart (to allow for expansion) on the lined baking sheets. Cover the sheets with a dampened tea towel or sheets of clingfilm and leave on the worktop to **prove** and rise for about 2–2½ hours, or until doubled in size. Towards the end of the rising time preheat the oven to 190°C (170°C fan), 375°F, Gas 5.

7. Uncover the buns and bake for 13 minutes, then reduce the oven temperature to 180°C (160°C fan), 350°F, Gas 4. Rotate the sheets, if necessary, so the buns colour evenly then bake for a further 5 minutes, or until the buns look golden brown and well-risen. Remove the sheets from the oven and quickly brush the tops of the buns with the 25g melted butter. Sprinkle with the 2 tablespoons demerara sugar and return the buns to the oven to bake for a further 2 minutes.

8. Transfer to a wire rack and leave to cool until just warm, then split and eat with butter.

Try Something Different

The same dough can be made into a large loaf. Punch down the risen dough, knead it for a minute then shape it into a loaf to fit a greased 900g (26 × 12.5 × 7.5cm) loaf tin (see page 19). Set the loaf in the tin then leave to rise as above. Bake for 40 minutes at 190°C (170°C fan), 375°F, Gas 5, then lower the oven temperature to 180°C (160°C fan), 350°F, Gas 4 and bake for a further 15 minutes. When the loaf is done remove from the tin and glaze the top with melted butter and sugar as above. Return to the oven for a further 2 minutes (bake directly on the shelf, not in the tin). Cool on a wire rack.

Pecan and Maple Spelt Loaf

Adding plenty of toasted nuts adds crunch as well as flavour, but the dough needs to be soft enough to easily incorporate them. The interesting shape of this loaf will allow you to practise your plaiting skills, although a round plait is far easier to create than it looks.

200g pecan halves
500g stoneground wholegrain spelt flour, plus extra for dusting
8g salt
7g sachet fast-action dried yeast
1 tablespoon rapeseed or olive oil
3 tablespoons maple syrup
about 300ml lukewarm water

1. Preheat the oven to 180°C (160°C fan), 350°F, Gas 4 and then toast the pecans in a baking dish for 8–10 minutes, or until just lightly coloured. Remove from the oven and leave to cool. (The oven can be turned off for now.)

2. Combine the flour and salt in a large mixing bowl, or the bowl of a free-standing mixer, then sprinkle the yeast on top and **mix** in with your hand. Make a well in the centre.

3. Add the oil, maple syrup and water to the well and gradually **work** into the flour with your hand or the dough hook attachment on slow speed to make a soft but not sticky dough. If the dough feels dry or there are dry crumbs at the base of the bowl work in more water, a tablespoon at a time. Stoneground wholegrain flours take longer to absorb liquid (become **hydrated**) than white flours so once the dough has come together leave the dough in the bowl, uncovered, for 5 minutes. If the dough has firmed up too much and feels stiff, work in a little more water. Only add more flour if it sticks to the sides of the bowl or your hands.
Continued

Easy does it

HANDS-ON TIME:
35 minutes

HANDS-OFF TIME:
2–2½ hours

BAKING TIME:
35 minutes

MAKES:
1 large loaf

SPECIAL
EQUIPMENT:
baking sheet

STORAGE:
Once cold, wrap the loaf tightly (whole or sliced) in clingfilm or put into a freezer bag and freeze for up to 1 month

4. Lightly flour your hands and the worktop and turn out the dough. **Knead** it thoroughly for 4 minutes, or for 2 minutes using the dough hook on slow speed, then scatter the pecans over the dough (there's no need to chop them up as they will become broken during kneading). Knead the dough for another 3–4 minutes (or 2–3 minutes with the dough hook) or until the nuts are evenly distributed and the dough feels elastic and pliable. Return the dough to the bowl, if necessary, and cover it tightly with clingfilm or a snap-on lid. Leave on the worktop to **rise** for 1–1½ hours, or until doubled in size. Line a baking sheet with baking paper.

5. Uncover the bowl and punch down (**knock back**) the risen dough to deflate it. Dust your hands and the worktop with flour again then turn out the dough. Knead the dough two or three times to shape it into a ball. Flour your fingers then flatten the ball to make a 24cm neat round disc. Using a sharp knife, cut the disc into three strips, attached at one end, then plait the three strips together.

6. Tuck the ends under then carefully transfer the loaf to the lined baking sheet. With your hands gently **shape** the sides of the plait so the loaf is rounded. Slip the sheet into a large plastic bag, trapping in some air so the plastic doesn't stick to the dough, and tie the ends. Leave to **prove** and rise on the worktop for about 1 hour, or until the loaf has doubled in size. Towards the end of the rising time preheat the oven to 220°C (200°C fan), 425°F, Gas 7, and put an empty roasting tin into the bottom of the oven to heat up.

7. When the dough is ready, remove the baking sheet from the bag and place it in the oven. Pour a jug of cold water into the hot roasting tin, to create a burst of steam, then quickly close the oven door and bake the loaf for 15 minutes. Turn down the temperature to 190°C (170°C fan), 375°F, Gas 5 and bake for a further 20 minutes until the loaf is a rich golden brown and sounds hollow when tapped underneath; it's a good idea to **test** the loaf after 10 minutes at this lower temperature and rotate the baking sheet if necessary so the loaf colours evenly. Transfer the loaf to a wire rack and leave to cool completely before slicing.

Baked Mocha Doughnuts

A quick and very easy way to make doughnuts that doesn't involve deep-frying or a yeast-based dough. The dough is simply stirred together and baked in a specially shaped tray. The crumb and crust are quite delicate just out of the oven, so handle gently.

2 teaspoons instant coffee (granules or powder)
4 tablespoons very hot milk
100g plain flour
30g cocoa powder
½ teaspoon baking powder
½ teaspoon bicarbonate of soda
good pinch of salt
125g caster sugar
2 teaspoons cocoa nibs
1 medium egg, at room temperature

2 tablespoons buttermilk or low-fat natural yoghurt
50g unsalted butter, melted, plus extra for brushing

To decorate
70g dark, milk or white chocolate, broken into pieces
10g unsalted butter
icing sugar, for dusting

1. Preheat the oven to 190°C (170°C fan), 375°F, Gas 5. Brush your moulds well with melted butter, paying particular attention to the raised centre. Pop the tray in the freezer or fridge for a couple of minutes just to harden the butter, then repeat (this double layer of butter works well with tricky mixtures).

2. Dissolve the coffee in the very hot (just below boiling point) milk then leave to cool until barely warm. Sift the flour, cocoa, baking powder, bicarbonate of soda, salt and sugar into a mixing bowl. Stir in the cocoa nibs.

3. Whisk the egg with the buttermilk (or yoghurt), coffee, milk and melted butter until thoroughly combined. Pour into the flour mixture and mix together with a wooden spoon.

4. Using a teaspoon, half-fill the prepared moulds with the soft, sticky mixture. (Keep any leftover mixture

to make more doughnuts after you've cooked the first batch.) Bake for about 17 minutes, or until well-risen and the doughnuts spring back when lightly pressed. Leave for a couple of minutes for the crust to firm up slightly, then turn out onto a wire rack to cool.

5. Melt the chocolate in a small heatproof bowl set over a pan of gently simmering water (make sure the bowl doesn't touch the water), stirring occasionally. Remove the bowl from the pan and stir in the butter. Leave to cool until thick enough to pipe. Spoon into a piping bag, snip off the end and pipe lines over the cooled doughnuts. Leave to set then dust with icing sugar.

Try Something Different

For a sweeter version, replace the cocoa nibs with 1 tablespoon of milk chocolate chips.

Easy does it

HANDS-ON TIME:
15 minutes

BAKING TIME:
17 minutes

MAKES:
6–8 doughnuts

SPECIAL EQUIPMENT:
6-hole non-stick large doughnut tray or 6 individual savarin moulds, small disposable piping bag

STORAGE:
Once cold, store in an airtight container and eat within 24 hours

Chocolate Breakfast Bread

The easiest of loaves – the dough is simply mixed and left to rise very slowly overnight, then gently shaped and baked in the morning. Because the mixture is so wet and sticky, and heavy with chocolate, fruit and nuts, keep a plastic scraper close by to help you move the dough around.

500g white spelt bread flour, plus extra for dusting
7g salt
10g caster sugar
¼ teaspoon fast-action dried yeast (from a 7g sachet)
100g dark chocolate, preferably a minimum of 70 per cent cocoa solids
100g pistachios, roughly chopped
125g soft-dried morello or sour cherries
425ml cold water

1. Put the flour, salt and sugar into a large mixing bowl and **mix** with your hand. Sprinkle the yeast into the bowl and mix in thoroughly.

2. Chop or break up the chocolate into large chunks – aim for 1.5cm but the exact size isn't crucial – and add to the bowl with the chopped pistachios and the cherries. Mix everything together, breaking up any clumps of fruit, using your hand.

3. Pour the water into the bowl, and using your hand as a paddle, **work** everything together until thoroughly combined to make a very heavy, very sticky wet dough. Take your time and check the base of the bowl as it is easy to leave some unmixed flour. Scrape the dough off your hand and cover the bowl tightly with clingfilm or a snap-on lid. Leave on the worktop to **rise** for at least 8 hours but no more than 12 (this is a wet dough so it can handle the longer rising time).
Continued

Easy does it

HANDS-ON TIME:
20 minutes

HANDS-OFF TIME:
9½ hours

BAKING TIME:
35 minutes

MAKES:
1 large loaf

SPECIAL EQUIPMENT:
900g loaf tin (about 26 × 12.5 × 7.5cm)

STORAGE:
Once cold, wrap (whole or thickly sliced) tightly in clingfilm or pop into a freezer bag and freeze for up to 1 month

4. The next day, uncover the dough: it will look well-risen and slightly bubbly. Grease the loaf tin with butter.

5. Lightly flour your hands and the worktop then turn out the dough. It will feel firmer though still soft and sticky. Using the dough scraper to help you, gently fold the dough in half and in half again.

Try Something Different

You can easily vary the flavours of this loaf: use a good-quality milk chocolate for a sweeter taste, replace the cherries with dried cranberries or raisins, or try chopped almonds or hazelnuts instead of pistachios.

6. Pat it out a little – it won't need much help – and repeat this folding procedure about six more times to make sure the chocolate, fruit and nuts are well distributed and the dough looks even. Try not to add any more flour as you do this.

7. Using the scraper, scoop up the dough and transfer it to the prepared tin. Press the dough into the tin so the corners are evenly filled, and the loaf has a regular, neat shape. Slip the tin into a large plastic bag, trapping some air inside so the plastic doesn't stick to the dough, and tie the ends. Leave on the worktop to **prove** and rise for about 1½ hours, or until the dough has risen to within 5mm of the top of the tin. Towards the end of the rising time preheat the oven to 220°C (200°C fan), 425°F, Gas 7.

8. Uncover the tin and bake the loaf for about 35 minutes, or until it is a good golden brown. To **test** if the loaf is fully baked, carefully turn it out and tap it underneath – if it sounds hollow the loaf is cooked, if not gently return the loaf to the tin and bake it for another 5 minutes and test again. Carefully set the loaf on a wire rack (the pieces of chocolate will be very hot, and the crust delicate until it cools). Leave until cold before slicing thickly and spreading with butter or creamy goats' cheese. Best eaten within 3 days.

Swedish Lussekatts

Baked for breakfast on 13th December each year, the dough for these sweet saffron buns is mixed with light cream plus butter and an egg, making it richer and heavier than other doughs. Avoid adding too much flour early on as the dough firms up after the second kneading, and allow longer than usual for it to rise.

1 teaspoon saffron strands
225ml single or whipping cream or Jersey high-fat milk, lukewarm
about 450g strong white bread flour, plus extra for dusting
10g fast-action dried yeast (from 2 × 7g sachets)
100g slightly salted butter
75g caster sugar
5g salt
45g raisins or sultanas
1 medium egg, at room temperature, lightly beaten

To finish
1 medium egg plus a pinch of salt, to glaze

1. Preheat the oven to 180°C (160°C fan), 350°F, Gas 4. Put the saffron into a ramekin and toast in the oven for 8–10 minutes, or until the strands turn a dark amber colour. Leave to cool for a minute then crumble into the lukewarm cream, stir well and leave to infuse for about 2 hours. (You can turn off the oven for now.)

2. To make the dough, combine 400g of the flour and yeast in a bowl and set to one side. Gently melt the butter and put into a large mixing bowl, or the bowl of a free-standing mixer. Reheat the saffron cream until it feels lukewarm when you dip in your little finger, then add it to the melted butter with the sugar, salt, dried fruit and the beaten egg and **mix** thoroughly with a wooden spoon.

3. Using your hand, or the dough hook attachment on slow speed, gradually **work** the flour/yeast mixture into the cream/egg mixture to make a very soft, slightly sticky, heavy and rich dough. Keeping the dough in the bowl (so you don't work in any more flour at this point) gently **knead** the dough for just 2 minutes – or 1 minute with the dough hook on slow speed. Cover the bowl tightly with clingfilm or a snap-on lid and leave on the worktop to **rise** for 1½–1¾ hours, or until doubled in size.
Continued

4. Uncover the risen dough and punch it down (**knock back**) with your knuckles to deflate it, then turn it out onto a lightly floured worktop. This time knead the dough thoroughly for 10 minutes, or 5 minutes with the dough hook on slow speed, working in just enough of the remaining flour until it feels satiny smooth, very stretchy and pliable, and soft but no longer sticky. The dough should hold a shape but not feel hard or dry.

5. Weigh the dough and divide it into 15 equal portions. Cover with a dry tea towel or sheet of clingfilm and leave the dough to relax on the worktop for 15 minutes. Line two baking sheets with baking paper.

6. One at a time, **shape** each portion into a ball then roll it back and forwards on an unfloured worktop with your hands to make a 21cm sausage.

7. Shape each sausage into a neat 'S' shape and arrange, spaced well apart, on the lined baking sheets. Cover loosely with sheets of clingfilm or a dry tea towel and leave to **prove** and rise on the worktop for 1–1½ hours, or until doubled in size. Towards the end of the rising time preheat the oven to 200°C (180°C fan), 400°F, Gas 6.

8. Lightly beat the 1 egg with a pinch of salt. Uncover the buns and very carefully glaze with the beaten egg – don't get the glaze on the baking paper as this will 'glue' the dough to it and stop the buns from expanding in the oven.

9. Bake the buns for 15–18 minutes, or until they are a rich golden brown; check them after 10 minutes and rotate the sheets, if necessary, so that they all colour evenly. Transfer to a wire rack and leave to cool slightly before eating.

Butternut Squash Loaf

Butternut squash, steamed and then blended to a smooth purée, replaces the liquid here and adds a sweet, earthy flavour to the bread. The gold-coloured dough is very soft and slightly sticky but firms up first as it is kneaded, then as it rises. Dried sour cherries and walnut pieces add texture and contrast to the rich sweet crumb.

Easy does it

HANDS-ON TIME:
35 minutes

HANDS-OFF TIME:
2 hours

BAKING TIME:
35 minutes

MAKES:
1 medium loaf

SPECIAL EQUIPMENT:
20cm round deep sandwich tin

STORAGE:
Once cold, wrap the loaf (whole or sliced) tightly in clingfilm or pop into a freezer bag and freeze for up to 1 month

about 600g butternut squash (unpeeled weight), peeled and cut into 2cm chunks
8g salt
30g unsalted butter, at room temperature
2 tablespoons caster sugar
¼ teaspoon ground allspice
¼ teaspoon freshly grated nutmeg
¼ teaspoon ground ginger

350–425g strong white bread flour, plus extra for dusting
7g sachet fast-action dried yeast
100g soft-dried morello or sour cherries
50g walnut pieces

To Finish
1 medium egg plus a pinch of salt, to glaze

1. Weigh out 400g of the butternut squash pieces (save the rest for soup or casseroles). Cook the squash chunks without any extra water – either in a steamer or in the microwave – until the chunks are just tender when pierced with the tip of a sharp knife, about 5–8 minutes. Leave to cool for 5 minutes, uncovered so the steam can escape, then tip into a food-processor.

2. Add the salt, butter, sugar, allspice, nutmeg and ginger and process to make a smooth, thick purée. Set to one side until lukewarm.

3. Put 350g white bread flour into a large mixing bowl, or the bowl of a free-standing mixer, and mix in the yeast using your hand. Add the lukewarm squash purée to the bowl and **mix** everything together with your

hand, or the dough hook attachment of the mixer on slow speed, to make a soft and slightly sticky dough. Depending on the type of squash, you may need to **work** in more flour to make a dough that is soft but doesn't stick to the sides of the bowl (some squash contain more water than others).

4. Scrape out the dough onto a lightly floured worktop and **knead** thoroughly until pliable and slightly firmer – about 10 minutes, or 5 minutes with the dough hook on slow speed. Return the dough to the bowl, if necessary, then cover it tightly with clingfilm or a snap-on lid and leave to **rise** on the worktop for about 1 hour, or until doubled in size. Grease the tin with butter and line the base with a circle of baking paper.
Continued

5. Punch down (**knock back**) the dough to deflate it then turn it out onto a lightly floured worktop and press it out to a rectangle roughly 20 × 30cm with one short side facing you. Scatter the 100g cherries and 50g walnut pieces over the bottom half of the rectangle then fold the dough over to cover the fruit and nuts.

6. Fold the dough in half again then press it out to a rough 25cm square and fold it in half, and then in half again. Do this once or twice more until the fruit and nuts are evenly distributed, then gently **shape** the dough into a ball about 15cm across.

7. Set the ball in the centre of the lined sandwich tin then slip the tin into a large plastic bag, trapping in some air so the plastic doesn't stick to the dough, and tie the ends. Leave to **prove** and rise for about 1 hour, or until doubled in size. Towards the end of the rising time preheat the oven to 220°C (200°C fan), 425°F, Gas 7.

8. Uncover the loaf and gently press your thumb into the centre of the loaf to make a small hollow. Lightly beat the 1 egg with a pinch of salt and brush over the loaf to glaze it then, with the tip of a sharp knife or a razor lightly score the loaf into 12 wedges from the hollow down to the edge. Bake for about 35 minutes, or until a rich golden brown. **Test** if it is ready by tapping the turned-out loaf underneath: it should sound hollow. Transfer to a wire rack and leave to cool completely before slicing.

Try Something Different

The same dough can be shaped into individual rolls: once the fruit and nuts have been incorporated weigh the dough and divide it into 12. Roughly shape into craggy-looking balls and then set well apart on a lined baking sheet. Leave to prove as above until doubled in size then glaze and bake for 15–18 minutes.

Monkey Bread

Here a soft dough is rolled into small balls that are then dipped in melted butter and rolled in cinnamon, sugar and chopped pecans. The balls are piled higgledy-piggledy into a loaf tin to create a crazy-paving pattern when the loaf is sliced.

500g strong white bread flour, plus extra for dusting
8g salt
7g sachet fast-action dried yeast
50g unsalted butter, melted
225ml lukewarm milk
1 medium egg, at room temperature

To assemble
100g unsalted butter, melted
75g light muscovado sugar
1 tablespoon ground cinnamon
100g pecans, fairly finely chopped

Needs a little skill

HANDS-ON TIME:
60 minutes

HANDS-OFF TIME:
2 hours

BAKING TIME:
35 minutes

MAKES:
1 large loaf

SPECIAL EQUIPMENT:
900g loaf tin (about 26 × 12.5 × 7.5cm)

STORAGE:
Once cold, the loaf can be tightly wrapped in clingfilm or put in a freezer bag and frozen for up to 1 month

1. Combine the flour and salt in a large mixing bowl or the bowl of a free-standing mixer. Add the yeast, **mix** it into the flour and make a well in the centre.

2. Mix the melted butter with the milk and egg then pour into the centre of the flour. Using your hand or the dough hook attachment on slow speed, **work** the liquid into the flour to make a smooth, soft dough. If there are dry crumbs and the dough feels dry and hard to work, gradually add a little more milk, a tablespoon at a time. If the dough is very sticky, work in a little more flour, a tablespoon at a time.

3. Turn the dough out onto a lightly floured worktop and **knead** it thoroughly for 10 minutes, or 4 minutes using the dough hook on slow speed, until the dough feels firmer and very elastic and smooth. Return the dough to the bowl, if necessary, and cover tightly with clingfilm or a snap-on lid. Leave to **rise** in a warm room for about 1 hour, or until doubled in size. Grease the inside and the rim of the tin with butter.
Continued

Try Something Different

Replace the pecans with the same amount of chopped hazelnuts or walnuts. Try sprinkling a few chocolate chips in between the layers.

107

4. Uncover the bowl and punch down (**knock back**) the risen dough to deflate it, then turn it out onto a lightly floured worktop. Divide the dough into about 60 tiny pieces, each the size of a large cherry or marble, by pulling or cutting off the dough. Roll each piece into a ball – they do not have to be neat or exactly the same size.

5. To assemble the loaf: put the 100g melted butter into a small bowl. Combine the 75g light muscovado sugar, 1 tablespoon ground cinnamon and 100g pecans in a separate bowl and tip onto a large plate. Dip the balls of dough, one at a time, first into the butter, then roll in the sugar mixture and put into the prepared tin. The pieces don't have to be arranged neatly, and there can be gaps between them, but the tin should be evenly filled.

6. Bang the tin on the worktop a couple of times to settle the contents and then slip the tin into a large plastic bag and leave to **prove** and rise on the worktop for about 1 hour (depending on the room temperature), or until doubled in size. Towards the end of the rising time preheat the oven to 200°C (180°C fan), 400°F, Gas 6.

7. Uncover the loaf and bake for 35 minutes until a good golden brown. Run a round-bladed knife around the inside of the tin then carefully turn out onto a wire rack and leave to cool. Eat warm, thickly sliced, or toasted.

Chelsea Buns

A popular London treat since the eighteenth century; a supple and sweet dough is rolled out, spread with butter, muscovado sugar and dried fruit, then rolled up and baked in chunky slices. Take care when baking – the buns needs to be cooked through so they are moist but not soggy, but don't let them overbrown or they will be too hard.

Needs a little skill

HANDS-ON TIME:
45 minutes

HANDS-OFF TIME:
1 hour 40 minutes

BAKING TIME:
30 minutes

MAKES:
12 buns

SPECIAL EQUIPMENT:
brownie or roasting tin (not loose-bottomed) about 21 × 25cm

STORAGE:
Keep the glazed buns in an airtight container and eat the same or next day

about 175ml milk
60g unsalted butter
1 medium egg, at room temperature
450g strong white bread flour, plus extra for dusting
6g salt
40g light muscovado sugar
7g sachet fast-action dried yeast

For the filling
50g unsalted butter, melted
75g light or dark muscovado sugar
150g dried mixed vine fruit (raisins, sultanas, currants)

For the glaze
3 tablespoons milk
3 tablespoons caster sugar
3 tablespoons clear honey
10g unsalted butter
pinch of salt

1. Gently warm 175ml milk and the butter in a small pan over a low heat, just enough to melt the butter, then leave to cool until lukewarm. Add the egg to the mixture and beat lightly with a fork until combined.

2. Put the flour, salt and sugar into a large mixing bowl or the bowl of a free-standing mixer and **mix** well with your hand. Sprinkle in the yeast and mix in. Make a well in the centre.

3. Pour the milk mixture into the well and gradually **work** into the flour with your hand, or the dough hook on slow speed, to make a soft but not sticky dough. The dough must be firm enough to hold its shape, but not stiff or dry,

as it will be rolled out. If the dough sticks to your fingers or the bowl, work in more flour, a tablespoon at a time; if the dough feels dry and difficult to bring together, or there are crumbs in the base of the bowl, work in more lukewarm milk, a tablespoon at a time.

4. Turn out the dough onto a lightly floured worktop and **knead** it thoroughly for 10 minutes, or 5 minutes using the dough hook on slow speed, until it feels silky smooth and very pliable. Return to the bowl, if necessary, and cover tightly with clingfilm or a snap-on lid. Leave on the worktop to **rise** for about 1 hour, or until doubled in size. Lightly grease the tin with butter.
Continued

5. Uncover the bowl and punch down (**knock back**) the risen dough to deflate it, then turn it out onto a lightly floured worktop. Knead it a couple of times then lightly flour a rolling pin and roll out the dough to a perfectly neat rectangle that is 45 × 20cm. Make sure that the dough is of an even thickness with no thick edges.

6. Brush the 50g melted butter evenly over the dough rectangle. Combine the 75g muscovado sugar with the 150g mixed fruit and sprinkle over the buttered surface of the dough, making sure it is evenly distributed.

7. Starting from one long edge lightly roll up the dough without stretching it, rather like a Swiss roll, to make a neat even cylinder.

8. With a long and sharp serrated knife, cut the cylinder into 12 even slices – use a gentle sawing motion to avoid crushing the roll.

9. Arrange the slices cut side up in the prepared tin, with just a little space between them, in four rows of three. Cover the top of the tin with clingfilm and leave on the worktop to **prove** and rise for about 40 minutes, or until doubled in size (the buns will now be just touching). Towards the end of the rising time preheat the oven to 200°C (180°C fan), 400°F, Gas 6.

10. Uncover the tin and bake the buns for 22–25 minutes, or until a good golden brown. While the buns are baking make the glaze: put the 3 tablespoons milk, 3 tablespoons caster sugar, 3 tablespoons honey, 10g butter and a pinch of salt into a small pan. Set over a very low heat and stir until the sugar has completely dissolved – don't let the mixture boil.

11. As soon as the buns are ready, remove the tin from the oven and brush the sticky glaze over the buns. Return the tin to the oven and bake for another 5 minutes until glossy. Set the tin on a wire rack and run a round-bladed knife around the inside of the tin to loosen the buns. Leave to cool for 5 minutes, then carefully turn out the buns onto the wire rack and leave to cool before gently separating them.

Try Something Different

For a different flavour replace some or all of the vine fruits with chopped soft-dried apricots and dried cranberries.

Poppy Seed
Challah

This iconic loaf gets its distinctive taste from eggs, plus a light oil (either olive or sunflower). This sweeter version of the classic bread is made with more honey. It is shaped from four plaited strands and finished with two thin coats of egg glaze to give the characteristic rich, glossy chestnut crust.

Needs a little skill

HANDS-ON TIME:
35 minutes

HANDS-OFF TIME:
2½ hours

BAKING TIME:
40 minutes

MAKES:
1 large loaf

SPECIAL
EQUIPMENT:
large baking sheet

STORAGE:
Once cold, wrap the loaf tightly in clingfilm or put into a freezer bag and freeze for up to 1 month

700g strong white bread flour, plus extra for dusting
2 tablespoons poppy seeds
10g salt
7g sachet fast-action dried yeast
250ml lukewarm water
100ml light olive oil or sunflower oil
3 medium eggs, at room temperature
3 tablespoons clear honey

To finish
1 medium egg plus a pinch of salt, to glaze
2 teaspoons poppy seeds

1. Put the flour into a large mixing bowl or the bowl of a free-standing mixer, then add the poppy seeds and salt and **mix** in with your hand. Sprinkle the yeast into the bowl, mix thoroughly, then make a well in the centre.

2. Measure the lukewarm water into a jug then add the oil, eggs and honey and beat together with a fork until thoroughly combined. Pour the egg liquid into the well then gradually **work** it into the flour with your hand, or the dough hook attachment of the mixer on slow speed, to make a soft dough. The dough should not feel firm, tough, dry or hard, so work in more lukewarm water if necessary, a tablespoon at a time, until the dough feels soft and there are no dry crumbs in the bottom. Only work in a little extra flour if the dough feels very sticky and clings to the sides of the bowl – it will firm up as it is kneaded but you want it to hold a shape at this point.

3. Lightly rub the worktop and your fingers with vegetable oil then turn out the dough: this will help keep the dough soft as working in too much extra flour can make it tough or dry. Thoroughly **knead** the dough for 10 minutes until it feels firmer, very pliable, satiny smooth and elastic; use a dough scraper to help you move the dough around on the worktop. You can also knead the dough using the dough hook on slow speed for 5 minutes.

4. Return the dough to the bowl, if necessary, then cover tightly with clingfilm or a snap-on lid and leave to **rise** on the worktop for about 1½ hours, or until doubled in size. Line a baking sheet with baking paper. *Continued*

115

5. Punch down (**knock back**) the risen dough to deflate it then turn it out onto a very lightly floured worktop and knead once or twice just to bring it into a ball. Weigh the dough and divide it into four equal portions. Roll each portion into a neat ball, then cover with a dry tea towel (this will help prevent the dough from drying out and a skin forming). Take out one portion and roll it back and forwards on the unfloured worktop (you need a little friction here) into an even sausage about 40cm long. Repeat with the three other portions of dough then arrange them vertically in front of you, slightly apart. Pinch the four ropes firmly together at the end furthest away from you.

6. To make the four-strand plait: pick up the rope on the far left and run it under the two middle ones, then lift it back over the last one it went under. Now, pick up the roll on the far right and run it under the twisted two in the middle, then lift it back over the last one it went under.

7. Repeat until all the dough is plaited then pinch the ends of the rolls together at the base of the plait. Neatly tuck each end under then lift the loaf onto the lined baking sheet.

8. Slip the baking sheet into a large plastic bag, trapping in some air so the plastic doesn't stick to the dough, and tie the ends. Leave to **prove** and rise on the worktop for about 45–55 minutes, or until almost (but not quite) doubled in size. Don't be tempted to leave the loaf in a very warm place to speed it up as you risk losing the definition of the braid. Towards the end of the rising time preheat the oven to 220°C (200°C fan), 425°F, Gas 7.

9. Lightly beat the 1 egg with a pinch of salt. Uncover the risen loaf and, starting at one end, carefully glaze it with a thin, even coat of beaten egg glaze (take care not to glue the dough to the lining paper). Repeat so the loaf has had two coats of glaze then sprinkle evenly with the 2 teaspoons poppy seeds.

10. Bake for 10 minutes, then reduce the oven temperature to 190°C (170°C fan), 375°F, Gas 5 and bake for a further 30 minutes, or until the loaf is a rich chestnut brown and sounds hollow when tapped underneath; for the best results **test** after 20 minutes and rotate the baking sheet if necessary so the loaf colours evenly. Transfer the loaf to a wire rack and leave to cool completely before slicing.

Try Something Different

For a change of flavour replace the poppy seeds with the same amount of sesame seeds. This is a traditional dairy-free bread but you can replace the oil with 85g melted unsalted butter for a slightly richer taste.

Cheat's Chocolate
Brioche Buns

These lovely buns are a good introduction to enriched doughs but, unlike a 'true' brioche, the dough is made without eggs and only has two risings. The butter is also simply rubbed into the flour, rather than squeezed into the dough itself. Good dark chocolate chunks or a chopped-up bar will give a real Parisian taste.

Needs a little skill

HANDS-ON TIME:
50 minutes

HANDS-OFF TIME:
2 hours

BAKING TIME:
20 minutes

MAKES:
12 buns

SPECIAL EQUIPMENT:
dough scraper, baking sheet

STORAGE:
Once cold, pop the buns into a freezer bag or airtight container and freeze for up to 1 month

450g strong white bread flour, plus extra for dusting
7g salt
60g caster sugar
7g sachet fast-action dried yeast
150g unsalted butter, chilled and diced
225ml lukewarm milk
½ teaspoon vanilla extract
100g dark chocolate chips or chunks, preferably a minimum of 70 per cent cocoa solids
extra milk, for brushing

1. Put the flour, salt and sugar into a mixing bowl or the bowl of a free-standing mixer and **mix** well with your hand. Sprinkle the yeast into the bowl and mix in. When thoroughly combined add the pieces of butter and toss them in the flour to thoroughly coat them.

2. Using the tips of your fingers rub the butter into the flour until the mixture looks like fine crumbs – take your time, as it is important that there are no lumps of butter. Make a well in the centre.

3. Add the lukewarm milk and the vanilla to the well then gradually **work** it into the flour with your hand, or the dough hook attachment of the mixer on slow speed, to make a very soft and sticky dough.

4. Scrape out the dough onto a lightly floured worktop and **knead** it thoroughly for 10 minutes, or 5 minutes using the dough hook on slow speed. The dough will still be soft but will feel slightly firmer and less sticky – avoid adding extra flour if possible as this will toughen the dough. Use a dough scraper to move the dough around on the worktop.

Continued

Try Something Different

For a sweeter taste, use milk chocolate chips. For a more grown-up flavour, replace the dark chocolate chips with the same amount of cocoa nibs.

5. Scatter the 100g chocolate chips or chunks over the dough and knead for a couple of minutes until evenly distributed then return the dough to the bowl, if necessary. Cover the bowl tightly with clingfilm or a snap-on lid and leave to **rise** on the worktop for about 1 hour, or until doubled in size. Make sure the bowl isn't left in a warm or sunny spot, as you don't want the butter and chocolate to melt and make the dough greasy.

6. Turn out the dough onto a lightly floured worktop — there's no need to punch it down — and shape it into a ball. Weigh the dough and divide it into 12 equal portions. **Shape** each piece of dough into a ball, then cover them loosely with a sheet of clingfilm and leave to rest for 5 minutes. Line a baking sheet with baking paper.

7. Using your hands, roll each ball on the worktop to a neat, even sausage about 9cm long. Arrange the sausages 3cm apart on the lined baking sheet then cover loosely again with a sheet of clingfilm.

8. Leave to **prove** and rise on the worktop as before for about 1 hour, or until the buns have almost doubled in size. Don't worry if some of them are almost touching. Towards the end of the rising time heat the oven to 190°C (170°C fan), 375°F, Gas 5.

9. Uncover the buns and brush lightly with milk. Bake for 18–20 minutes until a good golden brown all over. Check after 14 minutes and rotate the sheet if necessary so the buns bake evenly. Transfer to a wire rack and leave to cool before pulling apart. Eat the same or next day.

Swedish Cinnamon Buns

Feather-light, sweet and warmly spiced buns are finished with a crunchy and sticky glaze. They are made in the same way as Chelsea Buns: here the dough is even richer and more like a light brioche, flavoured with a touch of ground cardamom and rolled up with a buttery, gentle cinnamon filling.

425g strong white bread flour, plus extra for dusting
7g sachet fast-action dried yeast
60g light muscovado sugar
5g fine sea salt
½ teaspoon finely ground cardamom (from about 12 pods)
about 225ml lukewarm milk
1 medium egg, at room temperature
75g slightly salted butter, softened

For the filling
100g slightly salted butter, softened
90g light muscovado sugar
1 tablespoon ground cinnamon

For the topping
50g walnut pieces
30g unsalted butter
2 tablespoons water
125g light muscovado sugar

Needs a little skill

HANDS-ON TIME:
55 minutes

HANDS-OFF TIME:
1¾–2¼ hours

BAKING TIME:
25 minutes

MAKES:
9 buns

SPECIAL EQUIPMENT:
baking sheet

STORAGE:
Unglazed buns can be packed into an airtight container and frozen for up to 1 month. Defrost thoroughly, then reheat in a hot oven for 5 minutes and glaze as below

1. Put the flour and yeast into a mixing bowl or the bowl of a free-standing mixer and combine with your hand or the dough hook attachment. Add the sugar, salt and ground cardamom and **mix** in. Make a well in the centre.

2. Put the milk and the egg in a jug and beat lightly with a fork, just until combined, then add to the well. Gradually **work** the liquid into the flour mixture with your hand or the dough hook on the slowest speed, to make a very soft dough; if the dough feels stiff and dry, or there are dry crumbs at the bottom of the bowl, work in more milk, a tablespoon at a time. Cut the butter into small pieces, add them to the bowl and work into the dough by squeezing the mixture through your fingers – it will feel soft and slightly sticky.

3. Turn out the dough onto a lightly floured worktop and **knead** it very thoroughly for 10 minutes, using as little extra flour as possible for kneading – the dough will firm up as it is stretched and worked and will feel silky smooth and much less sticky. If you are kneading the dough in the mixer using the dough hook it will take about 5 minutes on slow speed. Return the dough to the bowl, if necessary, then cover tightly with clingfilm or a snap-on lid and leave to **rise** on the worktop at room temperature for 1–1½ hours, or until doubled in size. If the dough is left in a warm or sunny spot it will become too soft and difficult to shape. Line a baking sheet with baking paper.
Continued

4. Uncover the bowl and punch down (**knock back**) the risen dough with your knuckles to deflate it, then turn it out onto a lightly floured worktop. Knead it gently for a few seconds to form a neat and smooth ball. Cover the dough with the upturned bowl and leave it to relax for 5 minutes while you make the filling.

5. Put the 100g softened butter, 90g light muscovado sugar and 1 tablespoon ground cinnamon into a bowl and beat well with a wooden spoon until smooth and spreadable.

6. Uncover the dough and roll it out with a lightly floured rolling pin to a neat, evenly thick rectangle 28 × 38cm. Spread the filling evenly over the dough with a palette knife.

7. Start to roll the dough up fairly tightly, like a Swiss roll, from one long edge. When you get to the end pinch the seam together firmly.

8. Flour a large, sharp serrated knife and gently cut the roll into nine thick slices. Arrange the slices cut side down in three rows of three on the lined baking sheet, so they are about 1.5cm apart.

9. Cover the slices very lightly with clingfilm and leave to **prove** and rise on the worktop for 40–50 minutes, or until almost doubled in size. Again, take care not to leave them in a warm or sunny spot or you risk the butter melting out and the buns losing their shape. Towards the end of the rising time preheat the oven to 190°C (170°C fan), 375°F, Gas 5.

10. When the buns are ready, uncover the baking sheet and bake for about 25 minutes, or until a good deep golden brown. Five minutes before the end of the baking time make the topping: put the 50g walnut pieces, 30g unsalted butter, 2 tablespoons water and 125g light muscovado sugar into a small pan and stir over a low heat until melted. Bring to a boil and bubble for a few seconds.

11. As soon as the buns are ready, set the baking sheet on a wire rack and quickly spoon over the sticky topping. Slide the buns, still on the lining paper, off the baking sheet and onto the wire rack. Leave to cool then gently pull apart. Eat warm the same day or the next day.

Jam-filled
Doughnuts

These doughnuts are filled in the traditional way, by sandwiching together two discs of dough, rather than injecting after frying. Deep-frying takes patience and care as the oil needs to be at a steady temperature to guarantee evenly cooked dough. You could try filling these with mincemeat instead of jam for a Christmassy treat.

225ml milk
30g unsalted butter
2 medium eggs, at room temperature
450g strong white bread flour, plus extra for dusting
6g salt
40g caster sugar
7g sachet fast-action dried yeast

about 2 tablespoons good-quality jam, such as raspberry, strawberry, black cherry or apricot
sunflower oil, for deep-frying
caster sugar, for dusting

Needs a little skill

HANDS-ON TIME:
60 minutes

HANDS-OFF TIME:
2 hours

COOKING TIME:
10 minutes

MAKES:
12 doughnuts

SPECIAL EQUIPMENT:
dough scraper, 6.5cm round cutter, deep fryer (or wok), cooking thermometer

STORAGE:
Best eaten as soon as possible after cooking

1. Place the milk and butter into a small pan over a low heat, just until the butter melts, then leave to cool until lukewarm. Add the eggs and beat with a fork until combined. Set aside until needed.

2. Put the flour, salt and sugar into a large mixing bowl or the bowl of a free-standing mixer and **mix** well with your hand. Sprinkle the yeast into the bowl and mix thoroughly. Make a well in the centre.

3. Pour the milk mixture into the well and gradually draw in the flour, using your hand or the dough hook attachment on slow speed, to make a very soft and slightly sticky dough. If the dough feels dry or there are dry crumbs at the base of the bowl, **work** in more milk, a tablespoon at a time; if the dough is wet or sloppy or very sticky, work in more flour, a tablespoon at a time (the dough will firm up as it is kneaded and again during proving so it should be soft at this point).

4. Scoop the dough out onto a lightly floured worktop and **knead** it thoroughly for 10 minutes, or 5 minutes using a dough hook on slow speed, until the dough feels silky smooth, slightly firmer and very pliable: use a dough scraper to help you move the soft dough around rather than using a lot of extra flour.

5. Return the dough to the bowl, if necessary, then cover tightly with clingfilm or a snap-on lid, and leave to **rise** on the worktop for about 1½ hours, or until doubled in size. Make sure that the bowl isn't in a warm or sunny spot, as the dough will be difficult to shape.
Continued

127

6. Uncover the bowl and punch down (**knock back**) the risen dough to deflate it, then turn it out onto a lightly floured worktop. Knead it a couple of times, just to shape it into a ball, then cover it with the upturned bowl and leave it to relax for 5 minutes.

7. Lightly flour a rolling pin and roll out the dough, using short, gentle strokes, until it is 7.5mm thick. Dip the 6.5cm round cutter in flour and stamp out rounds from the dough. Gather up the trimmings, re-roll and stamp out more rounds – you will need 24 in total.

8. Set about ½ teaspoon of jam in the centre of 12 of the rounds, then dip a pastry brush in cold water and brush the dough border, around the jam, to dampen it.

9. Cover each round with a second round, then carefully press and pinch together the dough edges to seal them thoroughly and prevent the jam leaking out during frying.

10. Set the shaped doughnuts well apart on a lightly floured worktop (or a tray) and cover lightly with a sheet of clingfilm. Leave to **prove** and rise for about 30 minutes, or until doubled in size.

11. When the doughnuts are ready, heat the oil for deep-frying in a deep fryer to 180°C, 350°F (you could also use a wok or a large, deep-sided pan). Gently and carefully lower the doughnuts, one at a time, into the hot oil; cook them in small batches so the pan isn't overcrowded. Fry for 4–5 minutes on each side until the doughnuts are a deep golden brown. Check the temperature of the oil between batches to avoid overheating. Remove from the pan with a slotted spoon and immediately roll in caster sugar. Leave to cool before eating.

Stollen

This rich and buttery cake-like bread, studded with fruit, nuts and citrus peel, has become a Christmas classic. The dough has three risings, so allow yourself plenty of time, and plan to bake a week or two in advance to give the loaf time to mature.

175g mixed vine fruit
50g chopped mixed peel
4 teaspoons brandy or dark rum
zest and juice of 1 small unwaxed lemon
3 green cardamom pods
about 150ml milk
good pinch of fresh nutmeg
300g extra-strong white bread flour, plus extra for dusting
5g salt
45g caster sugar

10g fast-action dried yeast (from 2 × 7g sachets)
3 medium egg yolks, at room temperature
115g unsalted butter, slightly softened
50g whole blanched almonds, lightly toasted and roughly chopped
100g white marzipan

To finish
50g unsalted butter, melted
icing sugar, for dusting

Needs a little skill

HANDS-ON TIME:
60 minutes

HANDS-OFF TIME:
4 hours

BAKING TIME:
35 minutes

MAKES:
2 medium loaves

SPECIAL EQUIPMENT:
dough scraper, baking sheet

STORAGE:
Wrap tightly in greaseproof paper and foil and store in an airtight container for up to 15 days.

1. Tip the mixed vine fruit and peel into a bowl, stir in the brandy or rum, mix well, cover tightly and leave to soak at room temperature overnight. The next day, add the grated lemon zest and juice. Stir well, then cover and leave to soak until needed, stirring occasionally.

2. Pound the cardamom pods using a pestle and mortar to release the seeds. Discard the husks and continue to pound the seeds until lightly crushed. Gently warm 150ml milk with the nutmeg and crushed cardamom seeds, remove from the heat and leave to infuse for 15 minutes.

3. Tip the flour, salt and sugar into a large mixing bowl or the bowl of a free-standing mixer. **Mix** well then stir in the dried yeast and make a well in the centre. Add the infused milk and egg yolks to the flour mixture and **work** in with your hand, or the dough hook

of the mixer on the slowest speed, to make a very soft and slightly sticky, heavy, dough that holds its shape. If the dough feels dry and firm work in a little more milk, a tablespoon at a time, but if the dough seems sloppy, work in more flour, a tablespoon at a time.

4. Turn out the dough onto a lightly floured worktop and **knead** thoroughly for 10 minutes, or 5 minutes using the dough hook on the slowest speed, until the dough feels firmer and very elastic. Return to the bowl, if necessary, and cover tightly with clingfilm or a snap-on lid. Leave in a warm place to **rise** for about 1½ hours, or until doubled in size. Line a baking sheet with baking paper.
Continued

5. Divide the 115g butter into small pieces and work it into the dough (while still in the bowl) with your hands, squeezing the dough between your fingers until it is completely amalgamated. Turn out the dough onto a lightly floured worktop and pat out to a rectangle about 1cm thick.

6. Scatter the fruit mixture and the 50g chopped almonds along the centre of the dough. Fold in the two long edges of the dough so they meet in the centre, then fold in the two short ends to the centre.

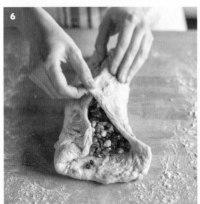

7. Fold the dough parcel in half. Lightly dust your hands and the worktop with flour, and pat out the dough and fold up as before two or three more times until the fruit and nuts are evenly mixed in. The dough will feel very soft and sticky but try to use as little extra flour as possible on the worktop and your hands, and use a dough scraper to move the dough around.

8. Return the dough to the bowl, cover as before and leave to rise at room temperature for about 1½ hours, or until doubled in size. Make sure the dough is not left in a very warm place or the butter will melt and ooze out.

9. Turn out the dough onto a lightly floured worktop then weigh it and divide in half. With floured fingers, pat out each piece to a rectangle about 16 × 14cm. With the side of your hand make a shallow groove down the centre of the dough parallel with the long sides.

10. Roll the 100g marzipan with your hands into a sausage 26cm long, then cut it in two and set one sausage into the long groove in each piece of dough.

11. Now fold each piece of dough in three – fold one long edge over to cover the marzipan, then fold over the other long edge to make a three-layer sandwich with the marzipan under two layers of dough (the top will have a 'hump'). Tuck the ends under neatly and transfer the loaves to the lined baking sheet, setting well apart to allow for expansion. If necessary, gently shape the loaves to make neat ovals.

12. Cover loosely with a sheet of clingfilm and leave to **prove** and rise at room temperature for about 1 hour, or until doubled in size. Towards the end of the rising time preheat the oven to 180°C (160°C fan), 350°F, Gas 4.

13. Uncover the risen loaves and bake for 35–40 minutes, or until a good golden brown. Check after 20 minutes and if necessary rotate the baking sheet and cover the loaves loosely with a sheet of baking paper if they seem to be browning too quickly.

14. As soon as the loaves come out of the oven slide them, still on the lining paper, off the baking sheet and onto a wire rack. Brush thoroughly and liberally with 50g melted butter and immediately dust with plenty of icing sugar. Leave until cold then wrap in greaseproof paper and foil and leave to mature for at least a week. Dust with more icing sugar just before serving, cut into thick slices.

Cinnamon
Swirl

A very pretty loaf, with a soft, rich crumb and sweet, spicy filling. The key to keeping a neat and even swirl with no gaps or holes is to use caster sugar rather than muscovado for the filling; caster sugar is finer and so melts more evenly. Take care when rolling and proving the loaf so it doesn't become misshapen.

125ml milk
125ml water
25g caster sugar
50g unsalted butter
1 medium egg, at room temperature
500g strong white bread flour, plus extra for dusting
8g salt
7g sachet fast-action dried yeast

For the filling
60g caster sugar
1 teaspoon strong white bread flour
1 tablespoon ground cinnamon
3 tablespoons milk, for brushing
small knob of butter, to finish

Needs a little skill

HANDS-ON TIME:
40 minutes

HANDS-OFF TIME:
1 hour 50 minutes

BAKING TIME:
40 minutes

MAKES:
1 large loaf

SPECIAL EQUIPMENT:
900g loaf tin (about 26 × 12.5 × 7.5cm)

STORAGE:
Best eaten the same day, or toasted the next day

1. Pour the milk and water into a small pan. Add the sugar and butter and heat gently, stirring, until the sugar has completely dissolved and the butter has melted. Remove from the heat and leave to cool until just lukewarm. Add the egg and beat with a fork until thoroughly combined.

2. Put the flour and salt into a large mixing bowl, or the bowl of a free-standing mixer, and mix well. Sprinkle the yeast into the bowl and **mix** thoroughly. Make a well in the centre.

3. Pour the milk/egg mixture into the well and gradually **work** into the flour with your hand, or the dough hook attachment on slow speed, to make a very soft but not sticky dough. If there are dry crumbs at the base of the bowl, work in more lukewarm milk (or water), a tablespoon at a time; if the dough sticks to the bowl, work in a little more flour, a tablespoon at a time.

4. Lightly flour the worktop and turn out the dough. **Knead** thoroughly for 10 minutes, or about 5 minutes with the dough hook on slow speed, until the dough is silky smooth, firmer and very elastic. Return the dough to the bowl, if necessary, then cover tightly with clingfilm or a snap-on lid and leave on the worktop to **rise** for about 1 hour, or until doubled in size.

5. Punch down (**knock back**) the risen dough to deflate it, then turn it out onto a very lightly floured worktop. Knead it a couple of times then pat it out to roughly a thick 18cm square. Cover it loosely with clingfilm and leave it to relax for 5 minutes – this will make the dough easier to roll. Meanwhile, grease the tin with butter and line the base and two short sides with a long strip of baking paper.
Continued

6. Combine the 60g caster sugar, 1 teaspoon strong white bread flour and 1 tablespoon ground cinnamon for the filling in a small bowl. Lightly flour a rolling pin and roll out the dough to a neat, even 26 × 48cm rectangle – make sure the sides are straight and the corners square. Brush the dough liberally with 2 tablespoons of the milk, then sprinkle with the sugar mixture in an even layer, leaving a 1cm border at one short end.

7. Roll up the dough, neatly and tightly, from the other short end and pinch the seam together to seal it firmly.

8. Lift the dough roll into the prepared tin, gently folding the ends under to make a neat shape. Slip the tin into a large plastic bag, trapping in some air so the plastic doesn't stick to the dough, and tie the ends. Leave on the worktop to **prove** and rise for about 50 minutes, or until just doubled in size – make sure the room isn't too warm as you don't want the dough to rise too quickly and become too big or the loaf will lose the neat swirl pattern and lose its shape. Towards the end of the rising time, preheat the oven to 180°C (160°C fan), 350°F, Gas 4.

9. Uncover the loaf and gently brush the top with the remaining tablespoon of milk. Bake for 35–40 minutes, or until the loaf is a good golden brown. To **test** if the bread is done, tap the base of the loaf – it should sound hollow; if there's a dull 'thud', return the loaf to the oven (set it directly on the oven shelf) and bake it for a further 5 minutes and test again. The loaf will have a soft and delicate crust so handle it carefully (the crust firms up as it cools).

10. Set the loaf on a wire rack and rub the top with a knob of butter on a scrap of kitchen paper (or butter wrapper), then leave until completely cold before cutting into thick slices.

Try Something Different

Use day-old slices of the loaf to make a delicious bread and butter pudding.

Kouign Amann

A traditional Breton yeasted pastry: the butter-rich laminated dough also has a generous amount of sugar folded in, which caramelises during baking to make pillow-like pastry puffs. There is no kneading involved here, so this is best made by hand to avoid the gluten developing.

Needs a little skill

HANDS-ON TIME:
50 minutes

HANDS-OFF TIME:
7 hours

BAKING TIME:
40 minutes

MAKES:
2 medium pastries,
to serve 8–10

SPECIAL
EQUIPMENT:
2 × 20cm deep round
sandwich tins (not
loose-bottomed)

STORAGE:
Best eaten the same
or next day

200g strong white bread flour, plus extra for dusting
50g plain white flour
5g salt
1 teaspoon golden caster sugar
7g sachet fast-action dried yeast
about 175ml lukewarm water

For the lamination
170g unsalted butter, chilled
140g golden caster sugar

To finish
2 teaspoons golden caster sugar

1. Put both flours, the salt and caster sugar into a mixing bowl and **mix** well with your hand. Sprinkle the yeast into the bowl and combine with the flour. Make a well in the centre.

2. Pour 175ml lukewarm water into the well and gradually **work** it into the flour, using your hand, to make a soft but not sticky dough. If there are dry crumbs in the base of the bowl, work in more water, a tablespoon at a time; if the dough feels wet and sticks to your hands or the sides of the bowl, work in more bread flour, a tablespoon at a time. As soon as the dough comes together in a ball stop working it – you don't want to develop the gluten, so there's no kneading involved here. Cover the bowl tightly with clingfilm and leave on the worktop, at normal room temperature, for 30 minutes. The dough will look a bit puffy but there is no need to punch down (**knock back**) here. Place the bowl of dough in the fridge for 2 hours.

3. Now prepare the **laminated dough**. Remove the dough from the fridge – it should look well risen and feel nice and chilled. Remove the butter from the fridge and place it between two sheets of baking paper. Pound it with a rolling pin until it feels pliable but cold.
Continued.

4. Scoop out the dough onto a lightly floured worktop – don't punch it down. Lightly flour a rolling pin and, using short light strokes, gently roll the dough in four directions to make four flaps around a thick diagonal central square. Set the butter in the centre and fold over the flaps to **enclose** the butter. Wrap tightly in clingfilm and chill for 1 hour.

5. Unwrap the dough, place on a lightly floured worktop and gently roll out, using light and short strokes, to a 54 × 28cm rectangle. Fold in three (fold the bottom third up over the middle third, then fold the top third down to make a three-layer sandwich of dough). Gently seal the edges then wrap in clingfilm and chill for 1 hour – this is your first '**turn**'.

6. Repeat Step 5 – this is your second 'turn'. Wrap and chill for 1 hour.

7. Unwrap the dough and this time, roll out to a 45 × 30cm rectangle. Sprinkle evenly with half the 140g golden caster sugar and gently press it onto the dough with the flat of your hand. Fold in three again – this is your third 'turn' – and wrap and chill for 1 hour.

8. Repeat Step 7, using the remaining sugar – this is your fourth 'turn'. This time, wrap and chill the dough for 30 minutes. Grease the tins with butter and line the bases with baking paper.

9. Unwrap the dough – it will measure 30 × 15cm – and cut it in half with a large sharp knife to make two 15cm squares. Gently roll each piece to a square to fit your prepared tins. Set a piece of dough into each tin; don't worry if they don't look very neat or

even-shaped as that is part of their charm. Loosely cover the tins with clingfilm and leave to **prove** and rise at normal room temperature for about 1½ hours, or until almost doubled in size. Take care not to leave the dough in a warm or sunny spot, as you don't want the butter to start to ooze out. Towards the end of this time preheat the oven to 200°C (180°C fan), 400°F, Gas 6.

10. Uncover the tins and sprinkle the dough with the 2 teaspoons golden caster sugar. Bake for 35–40 minutes, or until a rich golden brown, and bubbling. Carefully run a round-bladed knife around the inside of each tin to loosen the pastries and turn them out onto a wire rack. Leave to cool for 20 minutes before serving warm. These are best eaten warm the same or next day.

Kugelhopf

Traditionally baked for celebrations in Alsace, this tastes more like a cake, with the dough more closely resembling a cake mixture. It is baked in a deep fluted ring mould – the centre funnel means the cooking time is reduced, creating a delicate crust, so take care when unmoulding.

Needs a little skill

HANDS-ON TIME:
40 minutes

HANDS-OFF TIME:
2½–3 hours

BAKING TIME:
40 minutes

MAKES:
1 large loaf

SPECIAL EQUIPMENT:
20cm fluted kugelhopf or bundt tin

STORAGE:
Once cold, freeze (sliced or whole) in an airtight container for up to 1 month

For the tin
30g very soft unsalted butter
50g flaked almonds

For the dough
400g strong white bread flour
65g caster sugar
7g sachet fast-action dried yeast
200ml lukewarm milk
3 medium eggs, at room temperature, lightly beaten

finely grated zest of 1 large unwaxed lemon
6g salt
150g unsalted butter, softened
50g raisins
50g sultanas
50g flaked almonds
icing sugar, for dusting

1. First, prepare the mould (even if it has a non-stick coating): liberally butter the inside of the mould, particularly the centre funnel and the rim, then press the flaked almonds onto the sides and base so the inside of the mould is evenly coated. Chill, so the nuts are set in place, while you prepare the batter.

2. Put 150g of the flour and the sugar into a mixing bowl, and combine with your hand. Sprinkle the yeast on top and **mix** in. Make a well in the centre then pour in the lukewarm milk. Using your hand, draw the flour into the milk to make a smooth and thick batter. Cover the bowl with clingfilm and leave on the worktop for 1 hour.

3. Uncover the bowl – the batter will look 'spongey', with lots of small bubbles on the surface. Add the beaten eggs and the grated zest to the bowl and mix in with your hand. When thoroughly combined, gradually beat in the remaining 250g flour and the salt, using your hand like a paddle, to make a very soft and very sticky wet dough (it will be more like a thick batter than a regular bread dough).

Continued

143

4. This dough is too soft to knead in the usual way so the best way to develop the gluten is to beat the dough in the bowl by **slapping** it up and down with your hand. After 5 or 6 minutes it will feel firmer, very smooth and very elastic.

5. Cut up the 150g butter into small pieces and add them to the bowl. Squeeze the butter into the dough; once it has been incorporated slap the dough up and down a couple more times to make sure there are no streaks of butter.

6. Scatter the 50g raisins, 50g sultanas and 50g flaked almonds over the dough and gently squeeze it. Stop as soon as they are evenly distributed as you don't want the dough to become oily.

7. Spoon the dough into the prepared mould, taking care not to dislodge the flaked almond coating. Spread the dough so the mould is evenly filled – it should come about halfway up the sides.

8. Cover the top of the mould with a damp tea towel and leave to **prove** and rise on the worktop for 1½ –2 hours, or until almost doubled in size and about 3mm below the rim of the mould. Towards the end of the rising time, preheat the oven to 200°C (180°C fan), 400°F, Gas 6.

9. Uncover the mould and bake the kugelhopf for about 40 minutes, or until the top is a rich golden brown and a skewer inserted halfway between the rim and the centre funnel comes out clean. The baking time will depend on your mould (traditional ceramic and earthenware ones may take slightly longer than metallic ones), so check after 30 minutes and if the top seems to be browning too quickly, cover it with foil or baking paper.

10. Set the mould on a wire rack and leave to cool and firm up for 5 minutes before carefully unmoulding. Leave on the wire rack until completely cold then dust with icing sugar.

Try Something Different

For a festive dessert, whip 200ml double cream to soft peaks and use to fill the centre of the cold kugelhopf. Decorate with plenty of red berries and serve with a raspberry coulis, made by blitzing 200g fresh or frozen raspberries in a food-processor, straining to remove the seeds and sweetening with a tablespoon of icing sugar.

Hazelnut and Bitter Chocolate Babka

The dough for this babka is a rich, buttery challah made with eggs plus milk. The texture is crucial – here, coolness is the rule to prevent the butter oozing out of the soft dough so it is left in the fridge to rise slowly and firm up, and this makes shaping much easier. The bitter chocolate, muscovado sugar and nut filling is spread over the flattened dough then rolled up, to make two 'Swiss rolls', which are then twisted together.

Needs a little skill

HANDS-ON TIME:
60 minutes

HANDS-OFF TIME:
4–4½ hours

BAKING TIME:
50 minutes

MAKES:
1 large loaf

SPECIAL EQUIPMENT:
dough scraper, 900g loaf tin (about 26 × 12.5 × 7.5cm)

STORAGE:
Once cold, wrap in clingfilm and store in an airtight container for up to 5 days

400g strong white bread flour, plus extra for dusting
70g caster sugar
5g fine sea salt
7g sachet fast-action dried yeast
4 medium eggs, chilled
about 5 tablespoons milk, chilled
150g unsalted butter, slightly softened and diced

For the filling
150g dark chocolate, preferably about 70 per cent cocoa solids
50g light muscovado sugar
75g toasted hazelnuts
90g unsalted butter, melted

To finish
1 medium egg plus a pinch of salt, to glaze

1. Put the flour, sugar and salt into a large mixing bowl or the bowl of a free-standing mixer and **mix** well with your hand or the dough hook attachment. Sprinkle the yeast into the bowl and mix in, then make a well in the centre.

2. Break the eggs into a measuring jug, break them up with a fork without making them frothy, then add enough milk to make the liquid up to 265ml. Pour into the well, then gradually **work** the liquid into the flour, using your hand or the dough hook on the slowest speed, to make a soft and very sticky dough. If there are dry crumbs or the dough feels dry and tough, work in a little more milk, a tablespoon at a time.

3. Using a dough scraper to help, turn out the dough onto a lightly floured worktop and **knead** thoroughly for 10 minutes, or 6 minutes using the dough hook on the slowest speed. The dough will feel slightly firmer and more elastic. Gradually work in the butter, a few pieces at a time, to make a silky smooth, soft, but still sticky dough. As soon as all the butter has been incorporated, and you can no longer see any streaks, scrape the dough back into the bowl, if necessary, and cover tightly with clingfilm or a snap-on lid. Put the bowl into the fridge to **rise** for 2 hours, by which time the dough will have doubled in size.
Continued

4. Flour your knuckles and punch down (**knock back**) the dough. Re-**shape** it into a ball then cover the bowl tightly once more and return to the fridge for another hour. Meanwhile, grease the tin with butter and line the base and two short sides with a long strip of baking paper.

5. Turn out the dough onto a floured worktop and knead gently for 1 minute to make a neat ball. Cover with the upturned bowl while you make the filling.

6. Break up the 150g dark chocolate, put into the bowl of a food-processor with the 50g muscovado sugar and process to a fine rubble. Add the 75g toasted hazelnuts and pulse several times so they are roughly chopped.

7. Lightly flour a rolling pin and roll out the dough to an evenly thick rectangle, 30 × 40cm. Brush with two-thirds of the 90g melted butter to make a thick, even layer. Scatter the chocolate mixture over the top and gently press it onto the buttery layer with the flat of your hand. Drizzle the remaining butter on top.

8. Lightly score a line along the centre, to divide the dough into two 30 × 20cm sections. Starting from one 30cm edge, roll up the dough, fairly tightly, to the centre point. Repeat, starting from the other long edge, to make two rolls that meet in the middle.

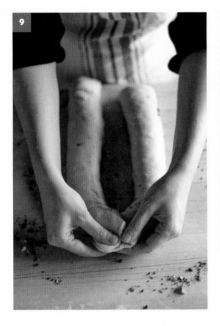

9. With a very sharp, long knife, cut along the line between the rolls. Pinch the cut edge of each roll to seal the seam, then pinch the two rolls together at one end.

10. Starting from the end you have just pinched together, twist the two strands together. Tuck the ends under and lift the twist into the prepared tin (a dough scraper might be helpful here); don't worry if it doesn't look neat – you can scoop up any filling that has escaped and sprinkle it around the twist. Don't pat or prod the dough twist – it will fill out the tin as it rises. Slip the tin into a large plastic bag, trapping in some air to prevent the plastic sticking to the dough, and tie the ends. Leave to **prove** and rise in a warm but not hot place (you don't want the butter to melt) for

1–1½ hours, or until almost doubled in size. Towards the end of the rising time, preheat the oven to 190°C (170°C fan), 375°F, Gas 5.

11. Lightly beat the 1 egg with a pinch of salt. Uncover the risen loaf and carefully glaze with the beaten egg. Bake for 45–50 minutes, or until a skewer inserted into the centre of the loaf comes out clean.

12. Set the tin on a wire rack, run a round-bladed knife around the inside of the tin to loosen the loaf, then leave it for 10 minutes before gently removing from the tin and placing on the rack – use the lining paper to help lift out the loaf as it will be quite delicate until it cools and firms up. Leave to cool completely before slicing and eating.

Croissants

Croissant dough is somewhere between a light, soft bread dough and crisp, flaky, butter-rich puff pastry. You'll need to plan to start work on these the day before to allow for chilling and rising times – follow the instructions carefully for best results. This recipe will take a bit of practice, even for an experienced baker, though once you've tasted home-made croissants you will be hooked, and ready to tackle larger projects, such as the Pains aux Cerises on page 176.

3 tablespoons caster sugar
10g salt
4 tablespoons milk powder
325ml cool water
500g white bread flour, plus extra for dusting
7g sachet fast-action dried yeast
250g unsalted butter, chilled

For the glaze
2 medium egg yolks, at room temperature
2 tablespoons milk

1. Add the sugar, salt and milk powder to the measured water and stir until completely dissolved. Put the flour into a mixing bowl or the bowl of a free-standing mixer, add the yeast and mix it in using your hand. Make a well in the centre, then add the milk liquid to the flour.

2. **Mix** everything together with your hand, or the dough hook attachment on the slowest speed, just until the ingredients are thoroughly combined to make a soft, slightly sticky and shaggy-looking dough, which comes away from the sides of the bowl – about 1 minute. Do not knead or overwork the dough at this stage as you don't want to develop the gluten.

3. Cover the bowl with clingfilm or a snap-on lid and leave in a warm spot to **rise** for 30–45 minutes, or until doubled in size. Gently punch down (**knock back**) the dough to deflate it, then re-cover and put into the fridge for at least 6 hours, preferably overnight; the cool, slow fermentation will boost the flavour as well as firm up the dough.

4. The next day prepare the **laminated dough.** Take the block of butter out of the fridge, set it between two sheets of baking paper and pound it with a rolling pin to flatten it. Re-shape into a brick and repeat the process a few times until the butter is cold and firm but pliable. Finally, shape the butter into a roughly 12cm square.

Continued

Needs a little skill

HANDS-ON TIME:
1¼ hours

HANDS-OFF TIME:
9¼ hours

BAKING TIME:
17 minutes

MAKES:
about 25 small croissants

SPECIAL EQUIPMENT:
2–3 baking sheets, croissant rolling cutter

STORAGE:
The shaped croissants can be open frozen at the end of Step 12 until firm, then tightly wrapped and frozen for up to 1 week. Defrost overnight in the fridge, or at normal room temperature for 4 hours, then continue with the recipe from Step 13

5. Turn out the chilled dough onto a lightly floured work surface. Punch down (knock back) the dough again, then **shape** into a ball. Cut a deep cross in the top of the ball and then roll out the dough using a floured rolling pin in four directions (making a quarter turn after each rolling), so the dough looks like a cross with a thick rough square of dough in the centre.

6. Set the butter on top of the rough square of dough, then fold the flaps of dough over the butter, tucking in the edges to completely **enclose** the butter so it doesn't ooze out during the rolling and folding processes. Cover with the upturned bowl and leave to rest for 5 minutes.

7. Lightly sprinkle the dough with flour then roll it out to a rectangle about 30 × 60cm; use short and quick movements to roll the dough, and take your time instead of using a lot of heavy pressure. Turn the rectangle of dough on its side so one long side is facing you. Fold in three – fold over the right third of dough (so it covers the centre portion) then fold over the left third to make a three-layer sandwich of dough. Use the rolling pin to seal the edges. Set the dough on a plate, cover tightly with clingfilm and chill for 40 minutes. This is your first '**turn**'. Line 2 or 3 baking trays with baking paper.

8. Repeat the rolling, folding and chilling process twice more, turning the dough a quarter turn to the left each time you start to roll.

9. After the third chilling, roll out the dough on a lightly floured worktop to a thin rectangle about 35 × 50cm. With a large, sharp, floured knife (or pizza wheel-cutter), cut the rectangle in half lengthways into two equal strips, each 17.5 × 50cm. Flour the knife or croissant rolling cutter and cut each strip into isosceles triangles with 17.5cm sides and a 7.5cm base – you should get about 12 triangles from each strip. If you are cutting with a knife, make a small cut at the mid-point of the base about 2cm long – this will help with the shaping. Stack the trimmings on top of each other, gently re-roll and cut another triangle or two (these won't look so good but they'll taste as nice).

10. Arrange the triangles on the lined trays, cover with clingfilm and chill for 10–15 minutes to firm up the dough and stop the butter oozing out in the oven.
Continued

Try Something Different

To make chocolate croissants, follow the recipe up to the end of Step 11. Break 100g good-quality dark chocolate (70 per cent cocoa solids) into small pieces and divide between the triangles, placing it near the centre of the base of each triangle. Roll up, shape and finish as in the main recipe.

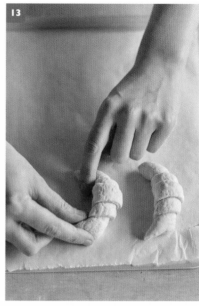

11. To shape the triangles, place them one at a time in front of you on a floured worktop. Gently stretch out the two shorter points (the cut at the base will help here).

12. Starting from the base edge, roll up the dough triangle: use one hand to roll the dough and the other to gently pull down the long point. Make sure you have the pointed end neatly in the centre of the shaped dough and underneath it so it keeps its shape in the oven.

13. Return the croissants to the lined trays, spacing them well apart, and gently shaping them so that the pointed ends curve inwards to make a curved crescent shape.

14. Lightly mix the 2 egg yolks and 2 tablespoons milk. Lightly brush the croissants with this egg glaze, taking care not to 'glue' the dough to the paper and working from the inside outwards so the layers of dough don't stick together and prevent the dough from rising properly. Leave in a warm but not hot place (you don't want to melt the butter) to **prove** and rise for about 1 hour, or until doubled in size. Towards the end of the rising time preheat the oven to 230°C (210°C fan), 450°F, Gas 8. The croissants are baked in a very hot oven to help the layers puff up and begin to set before the butter has time to melt; if the oven temperature is too low, or the croissant dough gets too warm before baking, the butter escapes and the dough starts to fry, with a tough rather than tender result.

15. Brush the croissants very lightly again with the egg glaze and bake for 10 minutes then lower the oven temperature to 200°C (180°C fan), 400°F, Gas 6 and bake for another 6–7 minutes, or until well-risen and a good dark golden brown. Don't undercook – unless the croissants are fully cooked before removing from the oven they will be heavy and soggy. Transfer to a wire rack and leave to cool. Best eaten the same day, although cooled, baked croissants can be wrapped in clingfilm, frozen for up to 1 month and reheated in an oven preheated to 180°C (160°C fan), 350°F, Gas 4 for 5–10 minutes.

Panettone

Panettone gets its fine, cake-like crumb from multiple rises: there's an initial batter-like 'sponge', followed by two rises before the dough is shaped, plus a final rise before baking, so set aside plenty of preparation time.

about 750g strong white bread flour, plus extra for dusting
2 × 7g sachets fast-action dried yeast
150g caster sugar
4 medium eggs, at room temperature
100ml lukewarm water
4 medium egg yolks, at room temperature
1 teaspoon vanilla extract
finely grated zest 1 large orange
finely grated zest 1 large unwaxed lemon

10g fine sea salt
350g unsalted butter, softened
100g large sultanas
70g candied orange and lemon peel, finely chopped
250g dark chocolate chunks or chips, preferably a minimum of 70 per cent cocoa solids
about 30g unsalted butter, to finish

HANDS-ON TIME:
1 hour 5 minutes

HANDS-OFF TIME:
6–7 hours

BAKING TIME:
1½ hours

MAKES:
1 large loaf

SPECIAL EQUIPMENT:
18cm (4.5 litre) loose-bottomed panettone tin or a very deep cake tin

STORAGE:
Leftover slices can be tightly wrapped in clingfilm and frozen for up to 1 month

1. **Mix** 250g of the flour with the yeast and sugar in a large mixing bowl or the bowl of a free-standing mixer, using your hand or the dough hook attachment. Make a well in the centre. Beat the whole eggs with the lukewarm water in a jug and pour into the well. With your hand, or the dough hook on the slowest speed, **work** the liquid into the flour to make a thick, smooth batter. Sprinkle about a tablespoon of the remaining flour over the top of the batter to prevent a skin forming, then leave in a warm spot for about 1 hour, or until the batter (sponge) has expanded and is bubbly.

2. Stir the egg yolks, vanilla extract and orange and lemon zest into the batter using your hand, or the dough hook on the slowest speed, then gradually work in 350g of the remaining flour plus the salt to make a soft and very sticky dough.

3. Cut the butter into small pieces and work it in by squeezing the dough through your fingers, or using the dough hook on slow speed, until thoroughly incorporated and there are no streaks.

4. Scoop out the dough onto a floured work surface and **knead** thoroughly for 10 minutes, gradually working in enough of the remaining flour to make a dough that is satiny smooth, very pliable and holds its shape. It should still be soft and sticky (but not wet or sloppy). You may not need all the flour, or you may need a little more. If you are using the dough hook, knead for 3–4 minutes on the slowest speed. Return the dough to the bowl, if necessary, and cover with clingfilm or a snap-on lid. Leave to **rise** at normal, or slightly warm, room temperature for 2–2½ hours, or until doubled in size. Don't leave in a very warm spot or the butter will begin to melt.

Continued

5. Uncover the bowl and punch down (**knock back**) the dough with your knuckles to deflate it, then cover the bowl and leave to rise as before until doubled in size – this time it'll take about 1½ hours. Meanwhile, combine the 100g sultanas with the 70g chopped candied peel and 250g chocolate chips or chunks in another bowl and toss with a teaspoon of flour so they don't clump together in the dough.

6. While you are waiting for the dough to rise, prepare the tin: grease the inside with a little melted butter and line the base and sides with a double layer of baking paper (or a single layer of parchment-lined foil). If you are using a deep cake tin rather than a special tall panettone tin, you will need to make sure that the paper around the inside of

the tin extends 8cm above the height of the tin. Wrap a folded newspaper around the outside of the tin, again 8cm above the rim of the cake tin, and tie in place with string. The long baking time means the outside crust can become hard and dry before the heat reaches the centre if the tin isn't well prepared, so don't be tempted to skip this bit.

7. Punch down (knock back) the risen dough, then turn out onto a floured work surface. Sprinkle the fruit and chocolate mixture over the dough and work in very gently with floured hands until evenly distributed. The dough will look glossy but no longer sticky. **Shape** the dough into a ball and gently drop it into the prepared tin.

8. With the tip of a long, sharp knife cut a cross in the top of the dough. Lay a sheet of clingfilm lightly across the top of the lined tin, without stretching it, and leave to **prove** and rise as before for 1½–2 hours, or until doubled in size. Towards the end of the rising time preheat the oven to 200°C (180°C fan), 400°F, Gas 6.

9. When ready to bake, set aside one-third of the 30g unsalted butter and melt the rest. Uncover the tin and brush half the melted butter over the risen dough to glaze, then put the remaining knob of butter in the centre of the cross. Bake for 20 minutes until just starting to colour, then brush again with the remaining melted butter. Return the panettone to the oven, reduce the temperature to 180°C

(160°C fan), 350°F, Gas 4 and bake for about a further 1–1¼ hours, or until it is a good golden brown and a skewer inserted into the centre comes out clean; start testing after 1 hour.

10. Remove the tin from the oven and stand it on a wire rack for 15 minutes to allow the crust of the panettone to firm up. Very gently unmould the loaf, peel off the lining paper, and set it on its side on the rack. Leave to cool completely before slicing. The loaf looks very grand served tied with a bright ribbon.

11. Serve panettone in thick slices with coffee or hot chocolate. It is best eaten within 3 days but is delicious toasted after that. Slightly stale panettone makes an excellent bread and butter pudding.

Brioche à Tête

Brioche is the finest, richest, most buttery and golden of breads. The delicate, sponge-cake crumb of a brioche is the result of three risings, so plan ahead and follow the instructions carefully. The rich, soft dough also needs to be thoroughly chilled before it can be shaped.

450g strong white bread flour, plus extra for dusting
10g salt
25g caster sugar
7g sachet fast-action dried yeast
4 tablespoons milk, chilled

5 medium eggs, chilled
250g unsalted butter, at room temperature, diced
1 medium egg yolk plus 1 tablespoon milk, to glaze

HANDS-ON TIME:
45 minutes

HANDS-OFF TIME:
5–5½ hours

BAKING TIME:
40 minutes

MAKES:
1 large brioche

SPECIAL EQUIPMENT:
large brioche mould, about 22cm in diameter across the top and 11cm at the base

STORAGE:
Once cold, the brioche can be tightly wrapped in a freezer bag and frozen for up to 1 month

1. Put the flour, salt and sugar into a mixing bowl or the bowl of a free-standing mixer and thoroughly combine with your hand. Sprinkle the dried yeast on top and **mix** in. Make a well in the centre.

2. Add the milk to the eggs in a measuring jug and beat with a fork, just to combine, then pour into the well in the flour mixture. **Work** the liquid into the flour, using your hand, or the dough hook attachment on slow speed, to make a very soft and very sticky, heavy dough.

3. **Knead** the dough in the bowl by **slapping** it up and down thoroughly for 10 minutes, or 6 minutes with the dough hook on slow speed, until it becomes glossy, firmer, smooth and very pliable.

4. Gradually work in the butter, a few pieces at a time, by squeezing it into the dough to make a silky smooth, soft and still sticky dough, with no visible streaks. If you are using a dough hook don't forget to scrape down the sides of the bowl every minute or so. Now, repeat the slapping/kneading for another 10 minutes (or 5 minutes using the dough hook on slow speed) – the dough should feel silky smooth and very elastic. Cover the bowl with clingfilm or a snap-on lid. Leave to **rise** on the worktop, at normal rather than warm room temperature, for about 1½ hours, or until doubled in size.

5. Punch down (**knock back**) the dough to deflate it, then re-cover the bowl and chill the dough in the fridge for at least 2 hours but not more than 6 hours. The dough should feel cool and firm but not hard. Meanwhile, liberally grease the brioche mould with butter. *Continued*

6. Turn the dough out onto a lightly floured worktop and **shape** into a ball. Cut off one quarter of the dough for the top and set it on one side. Reshape the remaining dough into a neat, smooth ball and set in the buttered mould.

7. Press your thumb and first two fingers together to make a pointed beak shape, then dip them in flour and press them into the centre of the ball of dough to make a deep hole (almost to the base).

8. Roll the reserved piece of dough into an egg shape, then shape and elongate the pointed end of this 'egg' so it fits into the hole in the larger ball. Using your fingers, gently insert the narrow pointed end of the 'egg' into the larger ball of dough, so the smaller ball sits neatly on top, dead centre.

9. Lightly beat the 1 egg yolk and 1 tablespoon milk together with a fork. Glaze the dough very lightly with the egg mixture, taking care not to let the glaze drip down the sides of the dough, or to let the dough become 'glued' to the mould, as this will stop it expanding evenly as it rises.

10. Slip the mould into a large plastic bag, trapping in some air so the plastic doesn't stick to the dough, and leave on the worktop to **prove** and rise at normal room temperature for 1½–2 hours, or until almost doubled in size, although this will depend on how long it was chilled for in Step 5. Towards the end of the rising time preheat the oven to 220°C (200°C fan), 425°F, Gas 7.

11. Uncover the risen dough and brush the brioche with glaze again. Dip a pair of kitchen scissors in cold water then snip all around the top of the dough between the rim of the tin and the centre ball of dough (you could make small slashes with a sharp knife instead).

12. Bake the brioche for 35–40 minutes, or until a rich golden brown. To **test** the brioche is properly cooked, carefully turn it out and tap it on the base – it should sound hollow. Check the brioche after 25 minutes and cover the top loosely with a sheet of baking paper if it seems to be browning too quickly. Set the unmoulded loaf gently on a wire rack and leave to cool completely before slicing.

Twisted Apricot and Almond Couronne

A rich soft dough, flavoured with orange, is spread with dried apricots, raisins and chopped almonds in a frangipane cream, rolled up then cut lengthways and twisted to reveal the many layers of dough and filling.

For the dough
225g strong white bread flour, plus extra for dusting
2 teaspoons fast-action dried yeast (from a 7g sachet)
4g salt
20g light muscovado sugar
finely grated zest of 1 medium orange
40g unsalted butter, at room temperature, diced
1 medium egg, at room temperature
75ml lukewarm milk

For the filling
100g soft-dried apricots
juice of 1 medium orange
85g unsalted butter, at room temperature
50g light muscovado sugar
1 medium egg yolk, at room temperature
60g ground almonds
¼ teaspoon almond extract
75g jumbo raisins
75g blanched almonds, lightly toasted

For the glaze
1 tablespoon caster sugar

HANDS-ON TIME:
55 minutes

HANDS-OFF TIME:
2½ hours

BAKING TIME:
30 minutes

MAKES:
1 large couronne, to serve 8–10

SPECIAL EQUIPMENT:
dough scraper, large baking sheet

STORAGE:
Wrap in clingfilm and keep in an airtight container overnight

To make the dough

1. Put the flour and yeast into a mixing bowl, or the bowl of a free-standing mixer and **mix** well. Sprinkle the salt, sugar and orange zest into the bowl and mix in thoroughly with your hand. Add the pieces of butter to the bowl and rub in using just the tips of your fingers, until the mixture looks like fine crumbs. Make a well in the centre.

2. Put the egg and milk in a measuring jug and beat with a fork until just combined, then pour into the well in the flour. Gradually **work** the liquid into the flour using your hand, or the dough hook attachment on slow speed, to make a very soft and slightly sticky dough. If there are dry crumbs in the bottom of the bowl, or the dough feels hard or a bit dry, work in a little more lukewarm milk, a tablespoon at a time.

3. Turn out the dough onto a very lightly floured worktop (try to use as little extra flour as possible as it's important to avoid the dough becoming tough or dry – a dough scraper will help you move the dough around) and **knead** it until the dough feels very pliable, firmer (though still soft) but no longer sticky – about 10 minutes, or 5 minutes using the dough hook on slow speed. Return the dough to the bowl, if necessary, and cover tightly with clingfilm or a snap-on lid. Leave to **rise** on the worktop for about 1½ hours, or until the dough has doubled in size. Line a large baking sheet with baking paper.

Continued

4. Meanwhile, roughly chop the 100g apricots for the filling, then soak them in the juice of 1 orange in a small bowl until needed.

5. Uncover the bowl and punch down (**knock back**) the risen dough to deflate it. Turn it out onto a worktop very lightly sprinkled with flour. Lightly flour a rolling pin and roll out the dough to a neat 30 × 22cm rectangle. Cover the dough lightly with a sheet of clingfilm and leave to relax while you make the filling.

To make the filling

6. Set a sieve over a small pan, pour the apricot mixture into it and leave to drain. Beat the 85g soft butter and 50g light muscovado sugar together in a bowl with a wooden spoon until creamy, then beat in the 1 egg yolk followed by the 60g ground almonds and ¼ teaspoon almond extract. Mix in the 75g raisins and the well-drained apricots (save the strained juice for the glaze). Finally, roughly chop the 75g toasted almonds and mix in.

To shape the couronne

7. Spread the filling mix evenly over the dough – take care that the fruit is evenly distributed – then roll up fairly tightly from one long side, like a Swiss roll. Pinch the seam to seal the roll. Dust your hands lightly with flour and very gently use them to roll the cylinder of dough backwards and forwards on the worktop, until it is 55cm long.

8. Flour a large, sharp knife and carefully cut the cylinder in half lengthways; try not to drag the knife as you want to keep the layers intact. Turn the two halves so the cut sides are facing up.

Continued

9. Gently twist both strands so the many layers are still visible, then shape the twisted dough into a ring. Pinch and twist together the ends neatly. Carefully transfer to the lined baking sheet.

10. Slip the tray into a large plastic bag, trapping in some air so the plastic doesn't stick to the dough, then close the ends of the bag. Leave to **prove** and rise on the worktop for about 1 hour, or until doubled in size. Towards the end of the rising time preheat the oven to 200°C (180°C fan), 400°F, Gas 6.

11. Uncover the risen dough and bake for 20 minutes, then reduce the oven temperature to 180°C (160°C fan), 350°F, Gas 4, and bake for a further 10–13 minutes, or until the ring is a good golden brown and firm to the touch (take care as the dough will be very hot). This sweet dough can easily 'catch', so check when you reduce the temperature and rotate the baking sheet if necessary so the ring bakes evenly.

12

To make the glaze

12. Set the baking sheet on a wire rack while you make the glaze: add the 1 tablespoon caster sugar to the reserved orange juice in the pan and stir over low heat until dissolved. Turn up the heat and boil rapidly for a minute to make a syrup. Brush this hot glaze over the ring then carefully slide the couronne, still on its baking paper, off the sheet and onto the wire rack. Leave to cool completely before slicing.

Try Something Different

- The almonds can be replaced with pine nuts or walnut pieces, and dried cranberries can be used instead of some or all of the raisins; try soft-dried peaches instead of apricots.
- For an extra sweet finish, make a water icing by mixing a few tablespoons of icing sugar with a little cold water, until you have a smooth, runny icing. Drizzle the icing over the ring in a zigzag pattern.

Mini Tropeziennes

If you started off baking scones to go with clotted cream and jam (see page 34), then mastered Devonshire Splits (see page 74), this is the grand finale, the ultimate teatime bun. Here, an even more buttery, sweet and feather-light brioche dough is stamped out into thick discs, which bake into small crunchy-topped buns. These are filled with a piped crème mousseline and decorated with fresh berries for a touch of the south of France!

For the sweet brioche

225g strong white bread flour, plus extra for dusting
5g salt
1½ tablespoons caster sugar
finely grated zest of ½ large orange
1½ teaspoons fast-action dried yeast (from a 7g sachet)
3 tablespoons cold milk
2 medium eggs plus 1 medium egg yolk, chilled
150g unsalted butter, at room temperature, diced
1 medium egg yolk beaten with 1 tablespoon milk, to glaze
about 2 tablespoons pearl sugar nibs, for sprinkling

For the crème mousseline filling

130ml creamy milk, such as Jersey high-fat milk
2 medium egg yolks, at room temperature
30g caster sugar
finely grated zest of ½ medium orange
10g cornflour
20g unsalted butter, at room temperature
1 teaspoon Grand Marnier or orange blossom water
50ml double cream, chilled

To decorate

225g small raspberries or strawberries

HANDS-ON TIME:
1¾ hours

HANDS-OFF TIME:
2½–3 hours +
6–12 hours

BAKING TIME:
15 minutes

MAKES:
10 tropeziennes

SPECIAL
EQUIPMENT:
dough scraper,
2 baking sheets,
6cm plain round
cutter, 1cm plain
round piping nozzle,
piping bag

STORAGE:
Once cold, the
unsplit and unfilled
buns can be packed
into a freezer
container and frozen
for up to 1 month

1. Start by making the sweet brioche. Put the flour, salt, sugar and grated orange zest into a mixing bowl or the bowl of a free-standing mixer. **Mix** well then sprinkle the yeast over the top and mix in. Make a well in the centre.

2. Put the milk, whole eggs and the egg yolk in a small jug and beat with a fork, just until combined. Pour into the well. Using your hand, or the dough hook attachment on slow speed, **work** the flour into the eggs to make a very heavy and sticky dough (it will stick to the sides of the bowl and your fingers).

3. **Knead** the dough thoroughly in the bowl by **slapping** it up and down with your hand, or with the dough hook on slow speed, until it becomes very smooth, slightly paler and firmer, and very elastic – this will take 10–15 minutes by hand, or 6–8 minutes with the dough hook.

4. Gradually work in the diced butter, a few pieces at a time, squeezing it into the dough through your fingers (or using the dough hook) to make a smooth, streak-free dough that feels softer and stickier; use a dough scraper to scrape down the sides of the bowl regularly. Repeat the slapping/kneading for 10 minutes (or 5 minutes with the dough hook) so the dough feels silky and elastic. Cover the bowl with a snap-on lid or clingfilm and leave to **rise** on the worktop, at room temperature, for 1½ hours, or until doubled in size.
Continued

5. Punch down (**knock back**) the risen dough to deflate it, then re-cover the bowl and put it in the fridge for at least 6 hours, preferably overnight, to thoroughly chill.

To make the crème mousseline

6. Meanwhile, make a crème pâtissière (the base of the crème mousseline). Gently heat the 130ml milk. Set a heatproof bowl on a damp cloth to stop it wobbling then add the 2 medium egg yolks, 30g caster sugar, finely grated zest of ½ medium orange and 10g cornflour and whisk (use a small hand wire whisk) for a couple of minutes then whisk in the warm milk. Tip the mixture back into the pan and whisk continuously over a medium heat until it boils and thickens.

7. Remove the pan from the heat and whisk in the 20g unsalted butter. When completely amalgamated whisk for another minute, until very glossy and smooth, then whisk in the 1 teaspoon Grand Marnier or orange blossom water. Transfer the mixture to a clean heatproof bowl, press a piece of clingfilm or dampened baking paper onto the surface and leave to cool. Cover the bowl tightly with clingfilm and chill for at least 6 hours or overnight.

To bake the sweet brioche dough

8. The next day, line two baking sheets with baking paper. Scoop the cold, firm brioche dough out onto a lightly floured worktop. Knead it once or twice – you don't want the dough to soften – then roll or pat it out to a thickness of 1.25cm (it should feel like shortcrust pastry). Dip the 6cm round cutter in flour then stamp out 10 rounds. Arrange them spaced well apart on the lined baking sheets (to allow for expansion) then cover lightly with sheets of clingfilm. Leave on the worktop to **prove** and rise at normal room temperature for 1–1½ hours, or until just doubled in size. Towards the end of the rising time preheat the oven to 190°C (170°C fan), 375°F, Gas 5.

9. Uncover the risen buns and glaze them very lightly with the 1 egg yolk and 1 tablespoon milk glaze (take care not to let the glaze run down the sides of the buns as this will prevent any expansion), then brush again with a second layer of glaze. Finally sprinkle with the 2 tablespoons pearl sugar nibs.

10. Bake for 12–15 minutes, or until the buns are a rich golden brown. Check them after 9 minutes and rotate the baking sheets, if necessary, so they all bake evenly. Transfer to a wire rack and leave to cool completely.

Continued

To assemble the tropeziennes

11. When you are ready to assemble, whisk the chilled crème pâtissière for a few seconds, just until smooth. Put a 1cm plain round piping nozzle into a piping bag. Whip the 50ml chilled double cream until it stands in stiff peaks, gently fold into the crème pâtissière, then spoon into the piping bag. Chill until needed. (You can also spread the crème if you prefer, using a palette or round-bladed knife.)

12. Split the buns in half horizontally. Holding the piping bag vertically pipe a small 'kiss' or button of the crème in the centre of each bun base. Pipe five more 'kisses' around this.

13. Take the 225g raspberries or strawberries and set a berry in the centre and between each 'kiss' (quarter or halve any large strawberries so they fit). Cover with the bun lids and serve as soon as possible.

Pains aux Cerises

These classic French buns are made from a yeast dough, laminated with butter in the same way as croissants (see page 150) to produce a luxurious combination of light, soft bread dough and crisp, flaky butter-rich puff pastry, plus dark, tangy cherries and sweet crème pâtissière. Take your time as this is quite an ambitious project, even for experienced bakers!

Up for a challenge

HANDS-ON TIME:
1¼ hours

HANDS-OFF TIME:
9–15 hours +
6–12 hours

BAKING TIME:
20 minutes

MAKES:
18 pains aux cerises

SPECIAL
EQUIPMENT:
pizza wheel-cutter
(optional), 2 baking
sheets

STORAGE:
Once cold, open-
freeze until firm,
then pack into
freezer bags and
freeze for up to
1 month

For the dough
35g caster sugar
10g salt
25g milk powder
325ml lukewarm water
500g unbleached white bread flour, plus extra for dusting
7g sachet fast-action dried yeast
250g unsalted butter, chilled

For the filling
200g soft-dried morello or sour cherries
3 tablespoons brandy or eau-de-vie (optional)

For the crème pâtissière
250ml creamy milk, such as Jersey high-fat milk
1 vanilla pod
3 medium egg yolks, at room temperature
50g caster sugar
20g cornflour
20g unsalted butter, at room temperature

To finish
1 medium egg yolk beaten with
1 tablespoon milk, to glaze

To make the dough
1. Add the sugar, salt and milk powder to the warm water in a measuring jug, stir well and leave for a couple of minutes until completely dissolved.

2. Put the flour into a mixing bowl or the bowl of a free-standing mixer. Add the dried yeast and **mix** it in using your hand or the dough hook attachment of the mixer. Add the milk mixture to the flour and beat with your hand, or the dough hook on the slowest speed, just until the ingredients are thoroughly combined to make a soft, slightly sticky and shaggy-looking dough that comes away from the sides of the bowl – about 1 minute. Do not knead or overwork the dough as you don't want to develop the gluten (this would make the dough stretchy but also tougher).

3. Cover the bowl with clingfilm or a snap-on lid and leave to **rise** in a warm spot for 30–45 minutes, or until the dough has doubled in size. Gently punch down (**knock back**) the dough to deflate it, then re-cover and put into the fridge for at least 6 hours or overnight to firm up.

To make the filling
4. Put the cherries in a bowl with the alcohol, if using. Stir well, cover and leave to soak until needed.
Continued

To make the crème pâtissière

5. Put the 250ml creamy milk into a medium pan, split the 1 vanilla pod lengthways and scrape the seeds into the milk. Chop the pod in half and drop the pieces into the milk. Place over a low heat until it just starts to come to the boil, then remove the pan from the heat and leave to infuse for 10 minutes (discard the pod pieces).

6. Set a heatproof bowl on a damp cloth, to stop it wobbling, and add the 3 egg yolks, 50g caster sugar and 20g cornflour. Whisk (use a small hand wire whisk) for a couple of minutes until very smooth, then whisk in the infused milk. Tip the mixture back into the pan and whisk it continuously over a medium heat until it boils and thickens – take care that the rich mixture doesn't catch on the base of the pan by adjusting the heat as you stir.

7. Remove the pan from the heat and whisk in the 20g unsalted butter. Transfer the mixture to a clean heatproof bowl and press a piece of clingfilm or dampened baking paper onto the surface to prevent a skin from forming. Cool, then cover the top of the bowl with clingfilm and chill for at least 6 hours or overnight.

8. The next day take the 250g block of butter out of the fridge, place it between two sheets of baking paper and pound it with a rolling pin to flatten it. Re-shape into a brick and repeat the process a few times until the butter is cold and firm but pliable. Finally shape the butter into a square with sides about 12cm.

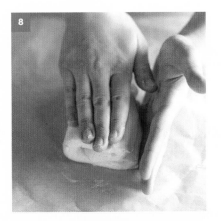

9. Turn the chilled dough out onto a lightly floured work surface. Punch down (knock back) the dough to deflate it, then shape the dough into a ball. Cut a deep cross in the top of the ball.

10. Roll out the dough using a floured rolling pin in four directions (making a quarter turn after each rolling) so the dough looks like a cross with a thick rough square of dough in the centre. Place the butter on top of the rough square of dough, then fold the flaps of dough over to **enclose** the butter, tucking in the edges so the butter doesn't ooze out during the rolling and folding processes. Cover with the upturned bowl and leave on the worktop to rest for 5 minutes.

Continued

11. Lightly sprinkle the dough with flour then gently roll out the dough to a rectangle about 30 × 60cm. Turn the rectangle of dough on its side so one long side is facing you. Fold in three – fold over the right third of dough (so it covers the centre portion) then fold over the left third to make a three-layer sandwich of dough. Use the rolling pin to seal the edges. Set the dough on a baking sheet, cover tightly and chill for 40 minutes. This is your first '**turn**'. Repeat the rolling, folding and chilling process twice more, turning the dough a quarter turn to the left each time you start to roll. Remember, this is a yeasted dough and also a puff pastry dough, so it's important to keep it cool enough for the butter to remain in layers within the dough and not start to soften and ooze out. Don't cut corners with the chilling

and resting times – if the dough begins to feel soft, cover and chill it until it is firm enough to start work again.

To make the pains aux cerises
12. After the third chilling roll out the dough to a thin rectangle about 50 × 34cm. Using a large, sharp, floured knife (or a pizza wheel-cutter), trim the edges to make a neat 48 × 32cm rectangle. Spread with the crème pâtissière then scatter the well-drained cherries over the top.

13. Starting from one short end, roll up the dough fairly firmly, like a Swiss roll, to make a thick roll about 33–34cm long (the dough stretches slightly as it is rolled up). Roll the roll onto a sheet of baking paper, making sure the seam is underneath. Lift onto a baking sheet or

a board, then cover lightly with clingfilm and chill until firm – about 1½ hours – this will make slicing easier. Meanwhile, line two baking sheets with baking paper.

14. Uncover the roll and, using a large, sharp serrated bread knife, cut into 18 slices, using a slow, gentle sawing motion.

15. Transfer the slices to the lined sheets, spaced well apart to allow for expansion. Use the tip of a small knife to tuck the end of each spiral slice underneath, and replace any cherries that have popped out. Gently push back into shape if necessary (any reshaped spirals will look fine after baking so don't worry). Lightly cover with clingfilm and leave on the worktop to **prove** and rise for 30 minutes, or until the spirals look slightly puffy. If your kitchen is very warm, or you

are baking in batches, move the sheets to the fridge. Towards the end of the rising time preheat the oven to 190°C (170°C fan), 375°F, Gas 5. These pastries are baked in a hot oven to help the layers puff up and begin to set before the butter has time to melt; if the oven isn't hot enough, the butter will escape.

16. Uncover the pains and gently brush with the beaten egg yolk and 1 tablespoon milk to glaze then bake for 18–20 minutes – they need to be a good golden brown for the best flakiness. Check after 15 minutes and rotate the sheets if necessary so they all bake evenly. Transfer the cooked pains to a wire rack. Best eaten the same or the next day – you can gently warm through at 180°C (160°C fan), 350°F, Gas 4 for 5–8 minutes.

What sweet bread or buns shall I bake today?

Conversion table

WEIGHT		VOLUME		LINEAR	
Metric	**Imperial**	**Metric**	**Imperial**	**Metric**	**Imperial**
25g	1oz	30ml	1fl oz	2.5cm	1in
50g	2oz	50ml	2fl oz	3cm	1¼in
75g	2½oz	75ml	3fl oz	4cm	1½in
85g	3oz	125ml	4fl oz	5cm	2in
100g	4oz	150ml	¼ pint	5.5cm	2¼in
125g	4½oz	175ml	6fl oz	6cm	2½in
140g	5oz	200ml	7fl oz	7cm	2¾in
175g	6oz	225ml	8fl oz	7.5cm	3in
200g	7oz	300ml	½ pint	8cm	3¼in
225g	8oz	350ml	12fl oz	9cm	3½in
250g	9oz	400ml	14fl oz	9.5cm	3¾in
280g	10oz	450ml	¾ pint	10cm	4in
300g	11oz	500ml	18fl oz	11cm	4¼in
350g	12oz	600ml	1 pint	12cm	4½in
375g	13oz	725ml	1¼ pints	13cm	5in
400g	14oz	1 litre	1¾ pints	14cm	5½in
425g	15oz			15cm	6in
450g	1lb	**SPOON MEASURES**		16cm	6½in
500g	1lb 2oz	**Metric**	**Imperial**	17cm	6½in
550g	1lb 4oz	5ml	1 teaspoon	18cm	7in
600g	1lb 5oz	10ml	2 teaspoons	19cm	7½in
650g	1lb 7oz	15ml	1 tablespoon	20cm	8in
700g	1lb 9oz	30ml	2 tablespoons	22cm	8½in
750g	1lb 10oz	45ml	3 tablespoons	23cm	9in
800g	1lb 12oz	60ml	4 tablespoons	24cm	9½in
850g	1lb 14oz	75ml	5 tablespoons	25cm	10in
900g	2lb				
950g	2lb 2oz				
1kg	2lb 4oz				

Index

Index

Acknowledgements

Hodder & Stoughton and Love Productions would like to thank the following people for their contribution to this book:

Linda Collister, Laura Herring, Alasdair Oliver, Kate Brunt, Susan Spratt, Joanna Seaton, Sarah Christie, Alice Moore, Nicky Barneby, Anna Heath, Damian Horner, Auriol Bishop, Anna Beattie, Rupert Frisby, Jane Treasure, Claire Emerson.

The author would also like to thank Barbara Levy, Laura Herring, Sarah Hammond, Nicky Ross, Clare Sayer, Jayne Cross, Laura Urschel, David Munns, Victoria Allen and Stevie Hertz.

First published in Great Britain in 2016
by Hodder & Stoughton
An Hachette UK company

1

Copyright © Love Productions Limited 2016
Photography & Design Copyright © Hodder & Stoughton Ltd 2016

A CIP catalogue record for this title is available from the British Library

Hardback ISBN 978 1 473 61555 7
Ebook ISBN 978 1 473 61556 4

Editorial Director: Nicky Ross
Editor: Sarah Hammond
Project Editor: Laura Herring
Series Editor: Linda Collister
Art Director: Alice Moore
Layouts: Nicky Barneby
Photographer: David Munns, Rita Platts
Food Stylist: Jayne Cross
Props Stylist: Victoria Allen

Typeset in Dear Joe, Mostra, Kings Caslon and Gill Sans
Printed and bound in Italy by L.E.G.O. Spa

Hodder & Stoughton Ltd
Carmelite House
50 Victoria Embankment
London EC4Y 0DZ

www.hodder.co.uk

CAERLEON

Continue on your journey to star baker with tips and advice on how to *Bake It Better* from the **GREAT BRITISH BAKE OFF** team.

DON'T JUST BAKE. BAKE IT BETTER.